□

The Architect
as Stand Designer

AXONOMETRIE (PLAFOND ENLEVÉ)

2429

ECHELLE 5cm P.M.

The Architect as Stand Designer

Building Exhibitions 1895-1983

DAVID DEAN

FOREWORD BY LORD REILLY   PREFACE BY H.B.G. MONTGOMERY

Published for the Building Trades Exhibition by
Scolar Press · London 1985

Published in 1985 in Great Britain for
the Building Trades Exhibition Limited by
SCOLAR PRESS
James Price Publishing Limited
13 Brunswick Centre
London WC1N 1AF

British Library Cataloguing in Publication Data
Dean, David, *1922–*
The architect as stand designer : building
exhibitions 1895–1983.
1. Building Trades Exhibition——History
2. Exhibitions——Booths——Design and construction
——History
I. Title   II. Building Trades Exhibition
725'.91   T396

ISBN 0–85967–713–3

Typeset by Gloucester Typesetting Services
Printed in Great Britain at the
University Press, Cambridge

Frontispiece. Venesta, 1930: Le Corbusier and
Perriand. *RIBA: BAL.*

☐
Foreword

by Lord Reilly

Although at first thought not about the most intri-guing subject in the world, this is a remarkably interesting book. It not only tells the story admir-ably of the birth and growth of the Building Trades Exhibition now known as Interbuild; it charts government attitudes to the building industry since government spokesmen, usually ministers, have come to accept as part of their duty the opening of each exhibition; it sketches the themes of each Interbuild; it describes in great detail the trend set-ting stands; it names their architects and designers. But it does much more than these, for David Dean is a man of rare discernment. As the Librarian of the British Architectural Library from 1960–83 he became familiar with the wheel of fashion in design; he became able to discern the ups and downs and to attach names to each swing of the pendulum; thus his account of the stands shown over the years becomes in miniature the story of British architecture over the same period. And, thanks to his admirable device of quoting from the professional press, he manages to ram home the message that architectural quality is the key. 'Quality talks across time,' said Richard Rogers at the RIBA when receiving his Royal Gold Medal for Architecture, and quality talks across exhibition halls to an audience of architects and builders, 'pro-fessionals with a design training that makes them particularly susceptible to a well-designed stand,

and particularly resistant to the rest' as David Dean writes in his introduction.

This account of the rise and rise of Interbuild is a powerful plea for the employment of qualified designers, whether architects or industrial design-ers, for from the very beginning of the Mont-gomery story names of architects and exhibitors appear which still command respect, while, as the years roll by, an increasing number of prominent architects are listed and illustrated – and how well illustrated. Indeed this book is a sort of roll of honour with almost all the great names appearing, and that is just what the Montgomerys of today would wish; but as David Dean points out these great names all appeared when they were young men and women, for exhibition stands, being ephemeral, are ideal projects on which young de-signers may cut their teeth. Equally, alas, they are ideal projects for second and third raters to try their hands at, so that the organisers of Interbuild have each year to accept a majority of stands 'assembled by' shopfitters or carpenters or others with no design training at all. But each time the organisers have the opportunity, which they seize with both hands, of designing the exhibition as a whole, its approaches, its lettering, its public face, so that each time Interbuild leaves its mark on the National Exhibition Centre and each Interbuild adds to the story of British design.

Contents

□

Preface

by H. B. G. Montgomery

In 1983 David Dean published his delightful book on Thirties architecture, and this coincided with his retirement as Librarian at the RIBA. The two events seemed to indicate that he would have time to work on a new book, and might also be prevailed on to interest himself in the subject of architects and exhibition stand design. We were lucky enough to persuade him that the task was not difficult, and that there was a wealth of published reference sources, which has served the building industry so well for more than a hundred years.

David Dean has produced just the sort of book we had been hoping for. It re-kindles old memories and also convinces us that a lot of exhibitors nowadays are missing very substantial benefits by not commissioning architects to design their exhibition stands as often as previously.

By using architects manufacturers of building materials benefit from what amounts to a practical consultancy programme on the use, both existing and potential, of the materials they are selling and portraying to the rest of their profession. They also get a stand that has a design input that will ensure that their products are critically noticed by other architects. Many a manufacturer in the past has also found that in the incorporation of his materials in his exhibition stand further information is often necessary and a more complete and useful selection of product literature results.

For the architectural practice the benefits are perhaps less immediately apparent, but the names in this book of some of those prestigious practices who have designed exhibition stands in the past should indicate some of the hidden values that can be found. And, as can also be seen from this book, the work of architectural practices is often more widely reported when the technical press discusses the design of their stands at building exhibitions.

Arising from the commissioning of a simple exhibition stand design there has often followed a long-standing consultancy agreement between the building material producer and the architectural practice, and this has resulted in the development of many new and exciting materials and new uses for existing materials.

Many architectural firms like the experience that designing an exhibition stand can bring to some of the younger members of the practice, and there is of course the dreaded time element which demands that the whole operation be finished at a certain time on a date well-known from the outset. This provides a sense of urgency and discipline that many other jobs do not have. It also encourages creativity and at the same time gives useful site experience to a young architect who may not otherwise find himself in such an all-encompassing management role for many years to come. It is also a comparatively clean job in that it has to be finished very quickly and not only completed, but also removed from the face of the exhibition hall. Not many architectural jobs vanish from the scene so quickly and completely, leaving behind only memories and references among architectural critics.

Just as taking part in international architectural competitions provides an agreeable sense of tension in an architectural practice, so too can participation in an exhibition. Even though the whole office may not be involved in the same way as it would be on a large site, there is nevertheless a possibility of a sense of community pride and also the opportunity of analysis over a short space of time, while memories are still fresh.

Many an architect has been surprised during the construction of an exhibition stand to observe stand-fitters' techniques and short-cuts. The intense feeling of speed and clamour brings not only its own problems, but also satisfaction in successful achievement.

From the organisers' point of view there is no doubt that the inclusion of a number of architect-designed stands in the exhibition enhances the visual appearance and excitement of the whole event. A building exhibition by its very nature has an audience that is very design-conscious, and the application of design intellect to the problems of marketing building materials has a substantial value for visitors and users of the exhibitions.

One of the dangers of growing old (and Interbuild is ninety years old this year) is that it seems that everything was better in the old days. Certainly, some things were easier in the past when there was a longer period available for build-up, the exhibition was open for longer, and people seemed to have more time just to stand and stare. Most of the exhibitions were hand-built and there was very little pre-fabrication of any kind. Nowadays, with the limited period of build-up and the greater realisation that time is money, far greater attention is paid to the less permanent aspects of exhibition display. However, there are still sufficient examples of architect-designed stands to show that the ingenuity of a trained designer can take the maximum advantage even of a short period of time and limited space so that their really creative uses of building materials and techniques can still achieve that sense of excitement which is so important at an exhibition.

We hope that this review of the past will encourage architects to examine the many advantages that they can achieve by designing exhibition stands. If more architects can make more contacts in this way with the building industry, then this publication will have achieved its purpose and we shall all again enjoy the delight which comes from visiting an exciting exhibition in an exciting industry.

Acknowledgements

Exhibition stands are ephemeral, the information about them fugitive. Designer or exhibitor may (but probably will not) have preserved pictures, but stands are hard to illustrate, and such pictures as do survive are not usually fleshed out with any account of how the stand really worked, what it actually looked like. So to search for information about stands of the past is all too often to pursue a will o' the wisp. When enough emerges to provide a basis for some minimal description, graphic and verbal, the writer cannot be sure that he has the *best* stand from that exhibition. He is dependent on the more or less fortuitous survival of description, and he wonders uneasily about the ones that got away.

Embarking on this account of nearly a century of stands would have been a barren task without the systematic reports, over most of that time, in contemporary periodicals. I have been heavily and gratefully reliant on these, as on the photographic libraries of the Architectural Press and The Builder Group. Their generosity (and the helpfulness of librarians Shirley Hind and Jane Roberts) must not be taken for granted simply because it is never failing.

In almost every case designers and manufacturers alike have been patient and helpful in the face of my enquiries, and I hope they will accept this scanty acknowledgement. But I must single out a few for particular gratitude: Neville Conder, Sir Philip Dowson, Roy Edwards of the Brick Development Association, Cecil Handisyde, Edward Mills, Beverley Pick, Tom Redgrove of British Gypsum, Gordon Ryder and John Stillman.

The Library of the Oxford Polytechnic and the RIBA's British Architectural Library made the book possible by their resources and their open access policy, and I owe the biggest debt of all to Andrew Millington, who did so much fruitful burrowing in libraries in the early stages of the work. Mrs Sue Warne typed my text impeccably; and finally my gratitude goes to everyone at the Building Trades Exhibition for help and encouragement, and to its Chairman Bryan Montgomery for giving me this opportunity to peer into a neglected corner where design and industry link hands.

11

Abbreviations

AA	Architectural Association	DRU	Design Research Unit
Archt	*The Architect*	DSIR	Department of Scientific and Industrial Research
A&BN	*The Architect & Building News*		
A&CR	*The Architect and Contract Reporter*	LCC	London County Council
A&BJ	*The Architects' and Builders' Journal*	MARS	Modern Architectural Research Group
ADes	*Architectural Design*		
AJ	*The Architects' Journal*	MOHLG	Ministry of Housing and Local Government
AP	Architectural Press		
AR	*Architectural Review*	MOPBW	Ministry of Public Building and Works
BAL	British Architectural Library		
BDA	Brick Development Association	NBEC	National Building Exhibition Company
Brit. Archt	*British Architect*		
Br. Bdr	*The British Builder*	NCB	National Coal Board
Bdr	*The Builder*	NEC	National Exhibition Centre, Birmingham
Bdrs' Jnl	*The Builders' Journal*		
Bdg	*Building*	RCA	Royal College of Art
BD	*Building Design*	RIBA	Royal Institute of British Architects
BN	*Building News*	*RIBA Jnl*	*RIBA Journal*
BS	British Standard	SCOLA	Second Consortium of Local Authorities
CLASP	Consortium of Local Authorities Special Programme		
		SIAD	Society of Industrial Artists and Designers
COI	Central Office of Information		
CPRE	Council for the Preservation of Rural England	TRADA	Timber Research and Development Association
DOE	Department of the Environment	ZDA	Zinc Development Association

Exhibiting by Design

The energetic prosperity of late Victorian Britain demanded a great deal of the building industry. Manufactures were surging; the 1870 Education Act and the 1875 Public Health Act had recognised social needs; commerce and domestic housing were responding to these needs; the population was increasing and towns were growing. All these factors created eagerly grasped opportunities for building.

It was high time to establish a shop window for the building industry. By the time H. G. Montgomery arrived to establish the Building Trades Exhibition in 1895 there had already been fifteen shows promoted by a body known as the National Building Exhibition Company. Admittedly they were quite unworthy. They may well have been kept going, and on an annual basis, more because they offered the paying public at the door all the fun of the fair than because they had much to interest the professional. Even the organisers talked about their 'mongrel display'.

Grumbling was not enough. The cure called for knowledge of the industry, energy, organising skills, a firm aim, long-term commitment to that aim, and sheer toughness. H. G. Montgomery, editor of *The British Clayworker* and dissatisfied exhibitor at the NBEC's exhibition in 1894, was the man the situation needed. He took charge, and continued to control and to shape the Exhibition for more than half a century.

The early stalls were literally that: the simplest of structures, equipped with counters and shelves, the goods neatly stacked in piles, and the whole thing usually adorned with much sign-writer's exuberance. But prompted by Montgomery, who was always keenly alive to aesthetic as well as commercial matters, some manufacturers rapidly made for the discipline which good design imposes and its consequent drawing power. As was to be shown by the 1909 stands by Lutyens for Daneshill (**13**) and Atkinson for C. H. Norris (**12**) and the Janus-faced Ravenhead stand of 1913 by Fair & Myer (**19, 20**), brick firms took the lead in producing imaginative stands (and in going to considerable architects for them). They were closely followed by the paint manufacturers, who explored the classical temple theme (like Purchase's stand for William Harland, 1913 (**16**)), where the brick firms concentrated on garden pavilions and, soon, on complete houses.

In the first thirty years the great mass of stands were not consciously 'designed' at all. Those that were mostly took existing kinds of buildings as their direct models. Through the 1920s designers grew bolder and more prepared to experiment; an exhibition was after all its own world and one that offered a huge variety of potential between the extremes of the trader's stall on the one side and the facsimile building on the other. A favourite theme, on which variations could be endlessly played, was the enclosed rectangular box (Carter (**34**) of 1926, Emberton's Thames Board (**40**) of 1928). Less usual was the unashamedly open stand like Atlas (**33**) of 1926, which reached its apogee in Le Corbusier's Venesta stand (Frontispiece, **42**) of 1930.

This was the only architectural work Le

Corbusier ever carried out in England. After fifteen days, at the exhibition's close, it was dismantled. But it symbolised the unmistakable arrival of modernism at the Exhibition, and in the next few years most of the leading modern figures, Wells Coates, Emberton, F. R. S. Yorke, Gibberd, Tecton, Fry among them, worked at Olympia. They were joined by architects from every part of the spectrum, for jobs were not abundant in the 1930s. But exhibition work was particularly important to the modernists, distrust of whose novel ideas and untried methods limited the range of commissions coming their way. However, on the strictly temporary stage of the Building Exhibition clients were far more willing to let them have their head, and this in turn resulted in a shop window for radical design and the effective use of new materials.

Few architects of any persuasion were too grand to take on work at the Exhibition, in the 1930s or at any time. At least fifteen Royal Gold Medallists for Architecture are known to have done stands – generally, it is true, well before receiving the profession's highest honour, but the fact speaks well for the manufacturers' ability to spot winners.

The diverse characteristics of 1930s architecture were all echoed at Olympia: the earnestness, the complacency, the light-heartedness and high spirits, and the social concern, the latter particularly in the series of special exhibitions within the Exhibition, organised by the Housing Centre: *New Homes for Old, Planning the Small Flat, Britain is Being Rebuilt*, all of which conveyed a strongly 'progressive' social message.

These displays were a sign of the organisers' determination to set exhibitions of building products and methods in an altogether wider frame, as were the shows of architectural drawings from the earliest days, and in recent years the complex range of seminars, led by distinguished people from right across the industry.

The exhaustion which followed the 1939–45 war made immediately post-war exhibitions displays of forbidden fruit (as the 1951 Festival of Britain could be seen as a dazzling display of what architects could do were it not for the inescapable restrictions). But these exhibitions were much more than that. They reflected, as they have always done, the economic pressures on society. As in the early 1920s 'substitute materials' were prominent, or in the late 1930s protection against bombing, so prefabricated components were a major post-war theme, to be followed by complete building systems, and in due course by the recent accent on rehabilitation and the improvement of the existing housing stock.

In the post-war years the stage was set for radical developments in exhibition design. The striking succession of government propaganda exhibitions during the war had laid the foundations and in the austere and idealistic days which followed a new professionalism was created. Architectural work was far from plentiful and some of the brightest new practices – James Cubitt, Lyons and Israel, Ryder and Yates, Edward Mills, Neville Conder, Stillman and Eastwick-Field – leapt at the chance of working at Olympia. So did another group, the young architects who were to make their special mark in design and exhibition work – Arcon, the Design Research Unit, Dewar-Mills, Stefan Buzas, Theo Crosby. At the same time the period saw the rise of a galaxy of non-architect professional specialists like Robin Day, Beverley Pick, James Gardner and Richard Levin. The arrival of all these talents made for a remarkable advance in the imaginative quality of stand design.

Another new element was the rise, about this time, of specialist exhibition contractors like Beck and Pollitzer and Fred Keil's City Display, with a host of lesser firms in their wake. The major companies, offering a whole range of services from finding a designer for the exhibitor to making and

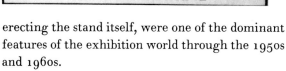

erecting the stand itself, were one of the dominant features of the exhibition world through the 1950s and 1960s.

Many of the stand contractors sought no more from the architect than an outline design, from which they constructed the stand, frequently re-using elements from previous stands they had worked on, and as time went by they gradually began to assume the crucial design role as well, with melancholy consequences for the stands' aesthetic quality.

In 1979 Owen Luder, shortly to become President of the RIBA and Chairman of the Exhibition, looked back in *Building* (30 Nov. pp. 50–51) over thirty years with what he called 'a nostalgic plea' for the old exhibitions he had known when he was 'a young, very green architect's assistant in the early 1950s . . . In those dreary work-starved years there was little scope for exciting design solutions.'

The Festival of Britain had shown how experiment in exhibition design 'could sharpen the creative edge, which could then be applied to more permanent buildings' and it was a real catch to be asked to do a stand in ideal conditions where you didn't have to worry about permanence or weather-proofing and were not handicapped by the growing regulations and restrictions which the architect met with outside.

His trenchantly expressed views provide, in passing, an interesting illustration of the way nostalgia can play the memory false. For him, he says, the Exhibition began to lose its attractions when it slipped from being an annual into a biennial event. But the fact is that apart from the years 1920 to 1922 (long before he was born) it has never been an annual show.

Luder was puzzled that exhibitors no longer held competitions for stand design. This was not only

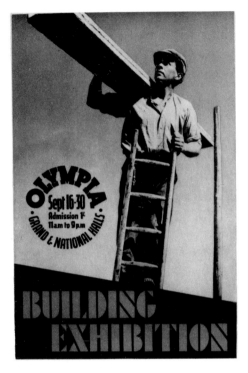

one of the best ways of uncovering young design talent, and not only quick, cheap and involving none of the cost, time and risk (to competitor and promoter) of the big competition; it was also 'a certain way for exhibitors, rightly or wrongly, to get more than their fair share of press coverage and attention'. To this list may be added the benefit to the clients of being able to take their pick among all the bright ideas submitted, not least on the most effective way of promoting their product.

Competitions can take various forms. As long ago as 1922 both H. G. Montgomery and *The Architects' Journal* held parallel 'ideas' competitions for stand design and layout. At the other end of the process are the recent Interbuild awards for the best stands in the current exhibition. But Luder of course was referring to manufacturers who put out to competition the design of their stand at the forthcoming exhibition. The great

years for this were the thirties and the fifties. In 1934 Skinner of Tecton won the Venesta competition (**51**); in 1936 Rodney Thomas began his association with Ascot by winning their competition (**67**). Ascot held another competition in 1955, won by Dennis Pugh (**91**), and other successful competitions were held by De La Rue in 1947 (winner Deryck Vesper (**75**)), by Crittall in 1949 and 1951 (each restricted to students, and won respectively by Frederick Rogerson of Liverpool University and by Group E from the Architectural Association), by Carter's (winner Nigel Lewis) (**99**) and by Sussex & Dorking Brick (winner W. H. Saunders and Son), both in 1959. The high rate of satisfaction they produced is shown by the way several of the exhibitors returned to their prize-winner for further designs in future years.

One of the signs of vigorous life at the Exhibition was innovatory experiment in conditions of very considerable freedom. This was so when Leathart was doing his series of stands for London Brick in the 1930s (**48, 61**), and Burnet, Tait and Lorne their British Steelwork Association stand in 1934 (**58**); it was emphatically so when James Holland and Peter Chamberlin did their sensational cantilevered stand for Lafarge Aluminous Cement in 1949 (**79**). But this was simply the most striking example among many of spirited design in the stands of the fifteen or so years after the war which made that period the high point of design in the Exhibition's history.

Undoubtedly manufacturers were prepared in the fifties to put substantial resources into the design and construction of their stands. John Stillman, of Stillman and Eastwick-Field, has said (in a letter to the author, 26 Sept. 84):

My own feeling during the years we were involved in these stands is that ours and many of the others were really too expensive to be built in Olympia for a relatively short exhibition. But then, we do not know what business they may have brought or what tax advantages there may have been. Certainly the firms seemed to stay in business.

In the 1960s the surge fell away. Many of the best architects and designers moved to bigger jobs. Manufacturers had other areas calling for funds at a time which was still insistent on economies. The advertising bans of professional bodies like the RIBA and the SIAD meant that speculative work was not possible; all had to be paid for, and contractors found it more economical to use their own designers. Indeed, many manufacturers economised both on designers and contractors by designing and building their own stands in-house, usually with discouraging results.

A notable development of the 1960s was the collaborative exhibit. There had been earlier instances, in Trystan Edwards's *The Silent House*, 1930, for example, and in Kenneth Lindy's *Design for Recreation* in 1949, sponsored by amenity societies, architectural schools and manufacturers. But it was in 1963 that the first of the major series of stands devised by David Rock and backed by manufacturers, trade associations and government departments made its appearance. This was *Industrialisation Interpreted*. Four years later came the most ambitious of all, *Componex*, in which the products of 260 companies, grouped in their building assembly context and described in a standardised format, were displayed over a five-level grid. This was followed in 1969 by a smaller collaborative display designed to provide information rather than to sell products, called *Profile of an Industry*.

These remarkable examples of large-scale co-operation had an unintended side-effect in persuading some manufacturers that it was more effective and economical to participate in big joint projects than to wrestle with individual design initiatives. For those still prepared to do so the arrival of the steel frame had a restricting effect. The frames were so straightforwardly efficient that they provided a natural starting point for the stand. Their widespread adoption reduced the scope for innovative excitement and gave the exhibitions as a whole something of a rectangular predictability.

This became more marked at the end of the sixties when shell stands were introduced. These were blocks of skeletal stands in which exhibitors leased individual units. Inside their units they had freedom for individual display, but only such freedom, of course, as the predetermined space and structure allowed. And it was a freedom which the exhibitor often passed on to one of the specialist firms of stand contractors who had spotted the gap and filled it by offering package deals.

Every exhibition produced its crop of fine stands, but overall the quality fell away as a direct consequence of the majority of exhibitors no longer going to architect-designers but resting content with the predictable sameness of stand contractors, whose capabilities did not necessarily include any very marked design talent. Still, there may have been some substance in the rumblings increasingly audible at the beginning of the 1970s that too much attention was paid to the stand at the expense of the promotion of the product, and fitness for purpose is significantly one of the criteria used by the Interbuild design awards panel which was set up in 1981.

But too much can be made of this. Cecil Handisyde (in a letter to the author of 19 Sept. 1983) sets out the view of the 1950s designer. 'The main target for a stand designer is to get people to notice the stand enough to go to it. Thereafter its products can be "sold" by the people on the stand.' Certainly the greater the stand's fitness for its purpose the better, but unless it hits Handisyde's simply expressed target it has failed and no amount of activity by 'the people on the stand' can retrieve the situation. Moreover, at the Building Exhibition a large number of those who must expressly be stopped from passing by the stand are professionals with a design training that makes them particularly susceptible to a well designed stand, and particularly resistant to the rest.

However, the Building Exhibition continued to thrive through the 1970s. It outgrew Olympia, and under its new name of Interbuild moved in 1977 to the much better designed and more spacious setting of the National Exhibition Centre in Birmingham. When the move took place, the building industry seemed at its lowest ebb, and few people would have been gloomy enough to forecast what was to follow. But in a setting of world unease and protracted recession the Exhibition continued to show a resilient flexibility, whether in promoting the drive for exports, especially in the Middle East, in meeting the new stress on rehabilitating the existing building stock or in grasping the implications of the communications revolution, from its 1960s outset in the shape of pre-classification and standardised trade literature to the vast potential of computer-aided design.

Stand design, the concern of this book, is only an aspect, however important, of the whole Building Exhibition picture. It is an aspect which has had its ups and downs through the years. At present it is not notably distinguished, in contrast to the Exhibition itself, now known as Interbuild, with 1,500 exhibitors from twenty-eight countries. Some reasons for the present character of stand design have been suggested, and the pendulum which started at the beginning of the seventies, very slowly but with increasing momentum, to swing away from the effectiveness and exhilaration of first-class design may soon begin to move back. If it does so, it will be to everybody's benefit. The only beneficiaries of the present position are those manufacturers who continue to put their trust in real design ability, for each exhibition shows that this ability is capable of producing results which are all the more potent and (literally) attractive for the prosaic nature of their surroundings.

The Agricultural Hall

Prehistory: From Bazaar to Building Exhibition

The Building Trades Exhibition has run in an unbroken line from 1895 to the present day. However, the exhibition which opened in the Agricultural Hall, Islington on the morning of 26 March 1895 had not sprung up fully armed out of nothing. There had been building exhibitions in the same hall for the previous fifteen years. But the similarity between this earliest series and its successors began and ended with the name.

The very first exhibition, in April 1880, proclaimed that its purpose was to display 'Architecture, Construction, Engineering, Furniture and Decoration, together with builders' plant of all kinds and sanitary appliances'. This was clear enough; but it turned out to be no more than a remote aspiration. The show was crammed with all manner of objects which had nothing whatever to do with building. Anyone with the stake money to hire a stall was welcome, and the results were more like a traditional fair than a trade exhibition.

It continued to run annually despite growing criticism and a widespread feeling that a fine opportunity was being lost. Leading the critics was the influential periodical *The Builder*. In 1892 it launched a strong plea that the exhibitions be less than annual, to allow proper time for planning, and that they should be controlled by a qualified selection committee.

The organisers themselves were plainly uneasy,

and in the following year the Honorary Secretary of the National Building Exhibition Company announced plans to hold what he himself called 'a *bona fide* Building Exhibition' in place of the present 'mongrel display' (*Bdr* 9 July 1893 p. 32). A committee was set up under the chairmanship of Banister Fletcher, Professor of Architecture at King's College London, now chiefly remembered for having created with his son, later Sir Banister Fletcher, the incomparable *History of Architecture on the Comparative Method*, that Gray's *Anatomy* of architecture, which, now in its eighteenth edition, still thrives.

Fletcher's committee reported good prospects for 1894 'despite the disfavour with which past building exhibitions have been regarded', and announced artisan competitions and a lecture series as ways of 'raising the tone of our annual exhibitions' (*A & CR* 16 Mar. 1894, p. 172). The repeated public hand-wringing by those concerned with running the exhibition indicates just how inadequate it was.

But the 1894 exhibition, though generally held to be an improvement, failed to demonstrate that the necessary clean sweep had been employed. It did not (said *The Builder*) 'bear out the very large promises made'. The catalogue was delivered a week late, and when at last it was available it was found to contain extended accounts of 'exhibits' which were not on display at all. It was being used simply 'to advertise wares which the exhibitors were not at the trouble to send' (*Bdr* 31 Mar. 1894, p. 252). There were strong objections too to the incessant touting. Clearly it was still a low-grade affair, and if the image of hucksters and hoop-la was ever to be overcome, an energetic and dedicated organiser was called for.

It was at this moment that the thirty-year-old H. Greville Montgomery appeared on the scene. He had been private secretary successively to the Liberal MP W. S. Caine, to Lord Yarborough and to the Duchess of Montrose, and he was to become a Liberal MP himself. He had (in the infelicitously worded comment of *Building News*, 22 Mar. 1895) 'found his feet in journalism with *Pearson's* . . . and has since made himself an honourable position'. When the Building Exhibition aroused his interest he was editor of *The British Clayworker* and was mounting a clay tile display. Not caring for the setting in which he found himself, he took forthright action, proposing to the NBEC organiser that the task should in future be shared. He himself would put up an equal stake on condition that he was given overall control. This was accepted; but when the day came for signing the agreement 'the organiser failed to turn up and I never heard any more of him. I decided to carry on alone' (interview with H. G. Montgomery, *Architectural Design* Sept. 1936 p. 371).

The involvement of Fletcher ('the moving spirit of my enterprise') was a great strength to him, and together with his brother H. C. Montgomery, known as Stow, he established a Consultative Council with Fletcher again in the chair. At once the pattern, which was to continue down the years, of close association with the architectural profession, displayed itself in the composition of the Council: Raymond Unwin, Blomfield, Waterhouse, Charles Barry the younger, E. W. Mountford, architect of the Old Bailey, and Fletcher's own son H. Phillips Fletcher, who was killed in the 1914–18 war.

1895

For the 1895 exhibition, the first under his aegis, Montgomery ordained that there were to be no hucksters, for popular appeal was not a major part of his objective. The aim was to provide a meeting place for the professions and the industry. Here they could make on-the-spot comparisons – and with foreign materials also: the Exhibition was seen as international from the start – and could gain a comprehensive view of current developments and likely future trends. One of his first decisions was to invite the President of the RIBA to become Chairman of the Exhibition, which became a tradition that still exists.

Under the new regime the Exhibition continued to take place in the Agricultural Hall, so that Montgomery's account (*Bdr* 12 Sept. 1930 p. 435) of setting to work to cleanse the Augean stables strikes home: 'I had to dispense with nauseous cattle-stalls left over from previous shows'. The main avenues of the Hall were filled with hansom cabs (a tribute, he suggested tongue in cheek, to their inventor the architect, MP and first editor of *The Builder* J. A. Hansom, though they were probably there simply to fill out the space). Cheap pince-nez, sticking plasters, marking inks, 'scents of wondrous odour' were all on offer, and he set to work to weed them out along with their undesirable exhibitors. His firm rule to exclude everything not relevant to the building trades

produced execrations from shooting gallery proprietors, optical lens dealers, watch makers, sweet stuff sellers and such like, who had hitherto reaped a fat harvest from the elite of Islington. Men used to come into the office and dangle gold sovereigns before one's eyes in the hope that the sight of gold might tempt one to relent, but it was to no avail. (*Bdrs' Jnl* 21 Sept. 1909 pp. 342–3).

It was a long job, but despite noise, haste and un-finished stands the exhibition opened on time and was acclaimed as far the best yet. No visual record seems to have survived, and critical comment centred naturally enough on the exhibits, among them names still familiar like Shanks and Potter-ton, rather than the stands, though the RIBA'S stand comes in for censure: 'it did not fulfil the expectations that might have been formed'.

Nor is there any evidence that architects were used, though among the wrought iron, decorated glass, marble and brickwork, there must have been some. There was 'a stand of drawings lent by the Institute of Architects', early indication that the Exhibition set its sights beyond simply the display of products, and *The Builder* comments tartly on a marble firm's stand showing 'a Celtic cross of some pretension which forms a prominent feature and would be better appreciated if it were not mounted the wrong way about'.

Not all was dedicated austerity however. The musical arrangements were specially commended, and they were on some scale. Miss Lilian Clausen's Pompadour Band consisted of 'some eighteen fair performers richly attired in the picturesque cos-tume associated with the spritely favourite of Louis XIV.' *The Builders' Journal* reports 'a little dinner of delicacy and reason' at the Cafe Royal with Banister Fletcher as host and some thirty RIBA members as guests, to celebrate the exhibition's success. The after-dinner oratory was 'inspiring', and the 'comfortable cordiality' of the occasion is hinted at by the report that Messrs Searles-Wood, Burrows and Benedict sang songs after a substantial number of toasts.

1897

At the 1897 exhibition the total of exhibitors leaped from about 90 to 220. Montgomery had put a stop to annual shows, settling on the biennial pattern which with one exception has been the custom ever since. At the same time he resisted suggestions from some quarters that five-yearly would be enough. That would be absurd, he said; they might depend on it, if it were to be held only once in five years a syndicate of businessmen would spring up 'and run a show simply for the gate money' (*A & CR* 9 Apr. 1897 Suppl. p. 19).

The 1897 exhibition was 'a technical display, not a fancy bazaar, as too many of these have proved in the past', wrote *The Builders' Journal*. Their own stand was the work of Waring the furniture purveyors, who were shortly to commission R. Frank Atkinson to design the Hampton Court baroque of Waring and Gillow's Oxford Street store. Their stand set an early example of what became a tradition at the Exhibition: a direct link with the fine arts. Its interior was enhanced with drawings by Pennell, Mallows and F. L. Griggs.

On display also was the architect J. P. Seddon's remarkable drawings cabinet, designed to show the unity of the arts and decorated with a series of panels depicting King René's honeymoon by Rossetti, Ford Madox Brown and Burne-Jones. And the Pilkington stand – Pilkington, like Aspinall's Enamel and Bratt Colbran, was among familiar names already exhibiting – included panels by Lewis F. Day and C. F. A. Voysey.

The exhibition was opened by the Lord Mayor of London, and again there was a celebratory dinner, this time given by the exhibitors to H. G. Mont-gomery. 'Speeches were commendably brief, and varied with sentimental and humorous songs,' commented a press report.

1899

The run-up to opening day has seen some tense scenes down the years, for even a single day's delay in achieving full preparedness can be seriously damaging. 1899 saw a hectic drive to complete on time, and one unsuccessful in some areas, so that the opening address of Professor Aitchison, PRIBA, whilst 'very interesting', was however 'owing to the noisy efforts of workmen and others putting the finishing touches to the stands, unfortunately inaudible to a large section of the audience' (*Bdrs' Jnl* 3 May 1899 Suppl. p. xcviii). Another journal speaks of 'the din and clatter . . . entirely drowning the speakers' voices', but it hails the results, saluting the taste displayed at the Exhibition and pointing out that it is comparatively easy to show decorative materials effectively, but quite another story with drainpipes and chimney pots (*A & CR* 28 Apr. 1899 p. 5).

The press in general were well disposed. 'We have never witnessed the opening of a more promising show, full of good things', said the *British Architect* (28 Apr. 1899 p. 301), and the stands themselves were specifically commended for 'their colour and artistic charms.' Meanwhile *The Builders' Journal* made play with a term fairly recently added to the language: there is 'as much jerry-building in the Agricultural Hall as in a growing London suburb. But this is a case in which jerry-building is positively virtuous and admirably ingenious' (26 Apr. 1899 Suppl. p. xc).

Among individual exhibits were a notable domed pavilion by Mural Decorations, deliberately left unfinished to expose its terra cotta and fibrous plaster construction and decoration, 'a symphony in green and yellow' from Jas. Gibbons, brass-founders and locksmiths, and a massive porch for Gibbs and Canning to display their glazed bricks, designed by

C. H. Townsend, who was working at the time on his design for the Whitechapel Art Gallery. Few other architects' names emerge, but their work within individual stands often appears, as in the carved chimney pieces and benches on John P. White's stand, by Mallows, Henry Wilson, Quennell and Voysey.

1901

In 1901 there was no formal opening ceremony, but instead a luncheon given to a large delegation of German brickmakers, who proposed the health of H. G. Montgomery 'with musical honours which astonished the Englishmen present.' But Montgomery was equal to the occasion, and called on 'his friends not to be outdone in lungpower, and with the assistance of the band of the Coldstream Guards they treated the Germans to a rendering of "For they are jolly good fellows" ' (*Bdrs' Jnl* 24 Apr. Suppl. p. xii). Besides the geniality, and the fortunate if rather surprising fact that the band of the Coldstreams happened to be on hand, what the episode shows is that the exhibitions had already acquired an international character; and further evidence was forthcoming in 1903 when there was a formal visit from the Union Céramique de France.

The Architect & Contract Reporter mounted a show of architects' drawings and thought well of it, comparing it favourably with the architecture section of the Royal Academy. *The Builder* however was dismissive: 'a not very large collection of perspective views and elevations, many of them already familiar . . . they need not detain us especially.' The display in question can be seen in the right foreground of what may be the earliest surviving general view of the Exhibition (7).

An acclaimed stand was that of Walter J. Pearce, designed by himself in the form of a truncated

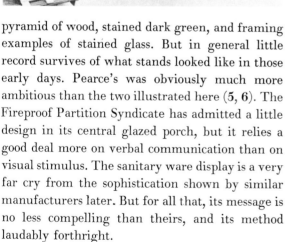

pyramid of wood, stained dark green, and framing examples of stained glass. But in general little record survives of what stands looked like in those early days. Pearce's was obviously much more ambitious than the two illustrated here (5, 6). The Fireproof Partition Syndicate has admitted a little design in its central glazed porch, but it relies a good deal more on verbal communication than on visual stimulus. The sanitary ware display is a very far cry from the sophistication shown by similar manufacturers later. But for all that, its message is no less compelling than theirs, and its method laudably forthright.

1903

The Exhibition grew steadily. By 1903 there were 250 stands. *The Builder* applauded its growth, but proposed that there should be less frequent exhibitions, open for longer. The paper was naturally aggrieved that its own critique was bound to appear too late to be of much use; there was no possibility of a preview, and since the exhibition ran for only eight days its published observations gave the reader just one day to follow them up. It was sharply critical too of the 'buttonholers' who thrust their papers uninvited on the visitor. If the managers, they suggested, would take a strong line in insisting that stand attendants give information only when asked, the tone and character would be raised above that of a bazaar. The organisers were very conscious of this problem. Among their counter-measures was a keenly appreciated notice: 'No Importuning in the Gangways'.

A drawings gallery was becoming an established feature, and on show this year were drawings by M. B. Adams, Maxwell Ayrton, W. D. Caroe, H. C.

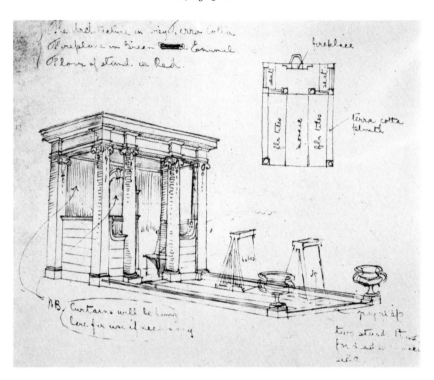

Florence, Ernest George, Morley Horder, Ernest Newton, Lewis Solomon and H. H. Statham. Press discussion centred on the admissibility (in contrast to the Royal Academy practice) of supplementary photographs, and on the cost of framing. In this last area H. Curtis Card's unenticingly captioned 'Seven Unsuccessful Drawings for the Harrogate and Knaresborough Infectious Hospital' were eloquent enough as they stood, unframed, of the risks of modern practice.

Designed, like so many early stands, within the company, George Wragge's display was hailed as 'a pleasant oasis' (*Brit. Archt* 19 Apr. p. 438). Clearly a bold venture in the Arts and Crafts manner displaying leaded glass, coloured plaster, smith's work, cast lead, electric fittings and the like, it avoided (said *The Builders' Journal* (17 June p. 263)) the 'strange treatments and phantasies of design so often carried (especially in Germany) to ill-

regulated extremes.' The firm's good taste showed its appreciation that 'novelty is not the sole aim even among moderns, and that a studied regard for design is more satisfactory than what some wild persons are pleased to call untramelled methods.' The *British Architect* weighed in too, applauding 'the decline of the extravagancies of *l'art nouveau* so far as the decorative part of the show is concerned', for though British designers had done some good work under this head, the general tendency 'in the hands of foreign artists has been unquestionably bad and unprincipled.'

1905

This frank admiration for the British way of doing things emerged again in the comments on the 1905 exhibition. The familiar difficulties made themselves felt in mounting the exhibition in time and in reconciling the need for high speed assembly with that for precision and scrupulousness in the display of products on the stands. 'On such occasions', purrs *The Architect & Contract Reporter* (28 Apr. Suppl. p. 19), 'the difference between English and foreign workmen becomes plain. One becomes excited by the novel circumstances, the other is as cool as if arranging stands in a hurry were his everyday occupation.'

One of the leading themes was that of fireproofing. An American exhibitor, Columbian Fireproofing, was one of several showing concrete fireproof floors, but in contrast to byelaws on the continent and in the United States British byelaws hindered the adoption of such systems. And they were not in themselves unreservedly welcomed. *The Architect & Contract Reporter* (21 Apr. Suppl. p. 3) granted the significance of such new materials but commented: 'According to some admirers concrete seems likely to supersede stone. That change will never take place in England – at least until our quarries are exhausted.'

Patent stone was much in evidence, and the Patent Victoria Stone stand was an early example of designing a bungalow with patent stone slabs. Other stands were more conventional. The Ripolin stand 'in the Adam style' was, said the press, 'a model of good taste . . . so successful that it merits preservation.' And the little Hall's Distemper stand was praised by the same journal: 'fitted up as a modern drawing room, the *tout ensemble* is a very pleasing example of that form of interior decoration which is coming so much into vogue in these days.'

The most interesting picture to survive from this exhibition is a sketch design (8) for the stand for Carter of Poole, a firm with a consistent record of good stand design down the years. The sketch shows a classical alcove in grey terra-cotta and within it an elaborate fireplace in glazed green faience. The floor is in red mosaic, and is edged with a terra-cotta plinth surmounted by two fine vases at the entrance.

Olympia

In 1905 there were 317 exhibitors and scores more were turned away. The size of the hall became an insoluble problem, and in 1907 the Exhibition moved to Olympia which was to be its home until 1977. The opening was performed by the Lord Mayor of London, Sir William Treloar, 'his genial presence and commanding figure meeting with appreciative comment at every turn' (*Bdrs' Jnl* 10 Apr. p. 162). In the course of his own address Sir Aston Webb PPRIBA spoke of the way exhibitions like the present one helped architects to overcome the many and increasing problems they faced. Instancing the begriming effect of smoke, he conjectured that in fifty years' time coal would be quite an out-of-date commodity, having been entirely supplanted by electricity.

One of the earliest stands for which the designer is known – indeed, and most unusually, he was named in the Catalogue – was that of C. H. Norris the brick firm (**10**). It is a little Georgian pavilion, designed to show the effects of broken colour in brickwork. The architect was R. Frank Atkinson, whose principal work was Waring and Gillow and the Adelphi Hotel in Liverpool, as well as interiors for the Cunarder *Transylvania* and the Pullman cars on the Brighton line. Although spoken of as 'a great attraction', it is less certain that a professional hand designed the stand for Associated Portland Cement. This was a square, white, open stand whose corner columns were decorated with photographs of buildings using the manufacturers' products. The stand's real attraction was perhaps the stage by stage display of the manufacture of Portland Cement, together with on the spot tests of the results to BS specifications.

A commentator in *The Builder* stressed the wisdom of using an architect to design stands: 'The Lithographic Stone & Marble Co. have a well-intentioned architectural erection in their material which, however, lacks the architect's hand' to give refinement to the detail. Likewise, Emdeca Decorations were 'not happy in their stand, which treats their material in a gewgaw manner ... they should have got an architect to design it for them' (*Bdr* 13 Apr. Suppl. p. 23).

Whether or not Newellite Glass Tile followed this advice, they produced a highly effective stand (**11**), an early example of the kind of display where the product is the stand. They showed a section of the new Underground extension from Euston to the Angel lined with their tiles and framing, beyond, a little octagonal pavilion in the Moorish manner.

The Builder's own stand was by W. Curtis Green, best known as designer of the Dorchester Hotel, and Royal Gold Medallist for Architecture in 1942. It was a simple kiosk with a latticed balustrade, the exterior decorated by lithographs from *The Builder*, the interior with original drawings by H. W. Brewer, A. N. Prentice and Curtis Green himself.

SIDE   FRONT

1909

In 1909 *The Builders' Journal* published (21 Apr. pp. 342–3) under the title 'The Outcome of an Idea' an account by H. G. Montgomery of the genesis and development of the exhibitions. In it he noted what he saw as their particular value:

they have stimulated the desire for things beautiful in the public mind, for whereas in past years the architect used to build houses without scarcely consulting his client, there is a tendency more and more to suggest to the architect ... The professional can see in the course of one or two visits what it would take him months to accomplish were he to travel the country in search of new and up-to-date ideas. Again, he can inspect the material as it appears in an actual building (and) he comes with the determination to talk business.

To these blessings A. W. S. Cross (whose son was to become PRIBA) added that the seductive claims of trade literature could be measured against the product itself.

Following his success in 1907 R. F. Atkinson again designed a brick pavilion for C. H. Norris (**12**). Its central square room had a brick-tiled floor and a domed plaster ceiling with cornice, and there was a brick-columned portico with a copper roof under a broken pediment with flanking wings roofed by trellis.

Walter Hoare of the Daneshill Brickworks commissioned from E. L. Lutyens another handsome garden pavilion, seen here, like the Norris pavilion, in a sketch by Raffles Davison (**13**). It was built entirely of Daneshill bricks, over which Lutyens had advised Hoare since the firm's founding five years previously. The bricks were small, handmade, hand-tempered Tudor-style, and burnt in old-fashioned Scotch kilns at Hoare's works in

Old Basing. They were at once a success, and had already been widely used, in work by Mallows, Eden, Phipps, Ernest Newton, and in at least eight houses by Lutyens himself, including Daneshill House which he built for Hoare in 1903.

1911

1911 saw an end to music at the exhibitions. Following complaints from some exhibitors that they were detrimental to business, bands were no longer hired to entertain the throng; things were becoming serious.

There was a good deal of press comment on the stands. Now that stand design was no longer left to the jobbing carpenter, said one journal, a visit to the exhibition 'is nothing short of a duty to the architect and an experience of genuine value to the builder.' Another called the exhibition 'remarkable for the costly manner in which many of the exhibitors fitted up their stands', whilst a third spoke glowingly about the quality of stand design, despite a few which 'without flattery may be described as absolutely and gratuitously hideous.' The same journal, despite the forthright manner of this comment, became rhapsodic in expressing its sadness at the brief life of what had given so much pleasure and so much instruction. Although the exhibition vanishes 'like snow upon the desert's dusty face, lighting a little hour or two, its soul must be born out of the living aims and hopes of those triple hundred stands . . . and its name is Progress.'

The design of a stand for a stone company dictated its own character much more readily than did that of, say, a floor finish manufacturer like Ronuk, which accordingly made use of the simple temple theme popular at this date (**15**). The exact positioning, however, within the surrounding balustrade,

12. C. H. Norris, 1909: R. Frank Atkinson. *Brit. Archt.*
13. Daneshill Brickworks, 1909: Edwin Lutyens. *Brit. Archt.*

of the four columns bearing the dome is puzzling, at least in the drawing shown here.

No such problems with United Stone Firms. Their stand (14) was an open pavilion with an Ionic screen and balustrade, each element of which used stones, from the firms' various quarries, different in colour and texture, and individually labelled. Nowadays there sometimes seems to be an open conspiracy in the press to omit wherever possible the name of a building's designer; but the practice is not new. Here *The Builder* contrived to note the names of the trellis purveyor, the electrical fittings supplier, the landscape effects painter, but not that of Ernest Runtz, who designed the stand itself. Runtz had been architect of the Gaiety Theatre in the Aldwych, though his own designs for the street frontage had been rejected in favour of Norman Shaw's baroque (now destroyed). This stand must have been one of Runtz's last works. His final years were clouded; a Horatio Bottomley libel action broke his son-in-law, and he himself, at his death in 1913 aged 54, is said to have been bankrupt.

An exhibit which attracted both attention and controversy was a model cottage designed by E. C. P. Monson for the builders Cornes and Haighton. Monson had an extensive practice centring on London municipal housing. His cottage had three bedrooms and cost £220 to build in brick (though the version shown at Olympia was constructed in concrete to speed erection time). It was denounced by *The Architect and Contract Reporter* (9 Dec. pp. 24–25) as 'doing a great deal of harm to the art of architecture and to honest building by implanting in the mind of the British public the idea that cheap and pretty houses may be obtained for almost nothing.'

Another target of the journal's anger was Thomas Parsons, paints, of Endell Street. They contrived an eye-catching model of the fore-part of a battleship, launched it under the name of HMS *Endelline,*

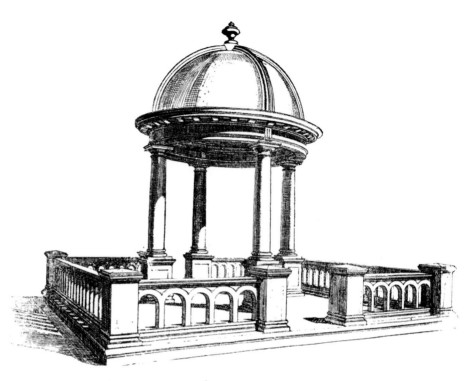

and continued ingeniously to use it until 1934 to show how admirably long-lasting was their enamel. *The Architect* was affronted; so histrionic an appeal to popular interest, it commented austerely, had no place in a business concern.

An effective way of promoting a product, which became popular in the twenties, was to give it immediacy by displaying it in actual current use. Crittall showed an early example in 1911 with 'the great steel windows being used at the new Whiteleys by Messrs Belcher and Joass.' Although the aesthetic aspects were not fully solved, said the *British Architect*, 'it is evidently the day of steel windows.'

1913

It was also the day of ferro-concrete, much in evidence in 1911 and still more so in 1913, when

The Builder insisted that the conservative objection that it called for specialist contractors was without foundation.

The same journal made two other comments which were to become familiar. It expressed a sharp regret that tariffs prevented so many of our best products being shown abroad, however cordial the invitations to display them, for the present duties transformed them into luxuries. It also initiated a debate which was to rumble on for several decades; could not, it asked, costs and labour at the Exhibition be reduced by a generally uniform treatment of stand space? This might inhibit individual flights of fancy, but it would give a unity to the whole. The stands mostly showed that designers had not taken proper advantage of opportunities. Whilst it agreed that products like brick were best shown in an independent structure, it would generally be cheaper to the exhibitor and 'more harmonious' to

the viewer were the promoters to lay out a standard pattern in which the exhibitors could simply take space. (*Bdr* 18 Apr. Suppl. p. 4).

Venesta, who were to use as designers at successive exhibitions in the thirties Le Corbusier, Wells Coates and Tecton, had the simplest of stands in 1913, which showed their art panels of photographs reproduced directly onto wood, and their Tudor oak panelling (1s. 3d. a square foot, including fixing and wax polishing).

Chief among brick displays was the stand of the Ravenhead Co. (**19, 20**). This showed the versatility of their bricks in a pavilion which was Tudor on two sides and classical on the other two, with Doric columns and a Babylonian winged lion on the flank in low-relief brick, a sculptural technique brought to its most attractive peak by the work of Walter Ritchie for the Brick Development Association in the 1970s. Ravenhead's pavilion was designed by

Fair & Myer, the latter of whom achieved fame fifteen years later as architect of the new Broadcasting House.

The quarry firms were also prominent. The stand of Penrhyn Quarries (**17**), by Reginald Fry, who had designed the Ideal Home for the *Daily Mail* the previous year, was intended to show how well different materials blended with slate in its various uses. It was designed as a complete cottage; under its slate roof, half-timber work was infilled with slate, the protruding piers were slate, the external floor paved with rough slate. Cecil Sharp's design for Oakley Slate Quarries (**18**) was broadly similar. Both of them, like so many of the more ambitious early stands, were intended to look as if they had always been there. But if the trick is really pulled off, the visitor may even feel a little diffident about intruding; would it not be unmannerly to disturb the gentleman at ease outside his cottage, reading

his newspaper? Still, the illusion of permanence belongs more to the drawings than to the built stand; it would hardly be sustainable in the hurly-burly of Olympia. Nearly half a century later a more sophisticated approach to stand design emerged, notably in the work of Theo Crosby, based on the recognition that a deliberately rough and ephemeral stand has its own appropriateness in an ephemeral exhibition.

Another favourite mode for stands was the classical temple. With its open frontispiece and flanks, this had the advantage over the enclosed cottage of allowing free sightlines through the site. A typical, and substantial, example was the temple designed by E. Keynes Purchase for William Harland (paints and enamels) (**16**) where the exterior was treated with flat enamel and the columns with glossy enamel, whilst the painted interior had in the hall a domed roof representing the heavens.

Only the Art Metal Construction Company broke away from the complete 'walk-in' structure, classical or vernacular, in favour of much open space on the stand, with a frontage down one side comprising a springing spiral staircase, metal grills, and between them lightweight hollow steel partition doors with fireproof glazing, designed by Mewès and Davis, architects of the Ritz Hotel and the Royal Automobile Club in Pall Mall. The whole stand was topped by typical and, to our eyes overbearing, lettered wooden panels.

21. Robert Kearsley, 1920: Hamptons. *AJ.*
22. *The Builder*, 1920. *Bdr.*

New World, New Start

1920

The first post-war exhibition, in 1920, gave a powerful impression of earnestness, of getting down to it, in contrast to what by then was seen variously as the ease, prosperity, extravagance or complacency of the old pre-war days. The new sense of urgency made inroads into many of the old attitudes, of the contractor against what he didn't understand, of operatives against the threat of unemployment, of architects against the feeling that fine building is incompatible with mechanisation.

So it was marked by the prominence of mechanical plant, shuttering, concrete mixers, standardised windows and the wide application of concrete in walls, roofs, doors, window frames, manhole covers. 'We certainly seem to prefer the concrete to the abstract', says a leader-writer in *The Architects' Journal* with uneasy jocularity. 'We are passing into an age of concrete. And that, whether we like it or not, seems the outcome of iron circumstances.'

Other dominant aspects were the development of new and substitute materials to overcome war shortages, the necessity for mass production (though, as *The Builder* observed, 'there must remain the scope and freedom to design the house'), and an impetus towards labour saving. This last was a response not only to the shortage and expense of domestic help, but equally to the shortage of trained operatives in the building trades and of traditional materials. Indeed, in his opening remarks, Dr Addison, the powerful new Minister of Health, asserted that the particular value of this exhibition was in its display of alternative materials and methods.

Off the peg houses were now available 'on outright purchase from the plans of well-known architects'; and the largest exhibit was that of British Everite and Asbestilite – a large two-storey timber-framed cottage (living room, three bedrooms, hall, scullery, kitchen, larder, washhouse) to illustrate the use of low-cost materials. It was erected in ten days, and, said H. G. Montgomery at the opening, it showed what could happen when developer, site owner, architect, builder and workman have a common interest. If it was possible in Olympia, he added, it should be possible to call on similar efficiency elsewhere to ease the critical housing shortage. Dr Addison agreed that it was a fine achievement, but cannily commented that it was one achieved regardless of expense. As it happened, heedless expense over housing was to be Addison's own undoing. As controller of Lloyd George's Homes Fit for Heroes campaign, he called on local authorities to put up unlimited numbers of houses and to let them at, in effect, controlled rents, government subsidy making up the shortfall. By the time the 1921 exhibition opened the huge expense of this had driven Addison from office.

Still, not all was austerity. There were temples, summer-houses, a Georgian panelled dining room, to say nothing of the unsinkable HMS *Endelline*. And there was a fine stand, by Hamptons, for Robert Kearsley the enamel firm (21): a semi-circular Doric colonnade enclosing a small domed

temple gazes across an open area – as spacious as it is welcoming, and sown with lawns, plants, flowers, even a tree – at another temple opposite, this time rectangular. Meanwhile another enamel firm, Pinchin and Johnson, showed an ambitious variation on Nelson's Column; an octagonal base surmounted by an Ionic column and topped by a globe, the whole guarded by four recumbent plastic lions.

The Builder stand (22) had become very plain. It had lost the trellised top originally given to it by Curtis Green in 1907 and was now no more than a bare shell for the display of drawings and engravings with an interior like a high-minded pub where copies of *The Builder* rather than beer were dispensed over the bar. There is no indication as to who designed it. Indeed, few names of designers survive from the exhibition, and it is symptomatic that even when *The Architects' Journal* published an

article under the title 'The Stands: an architect's view', its author commended thirteen stands but recorded the designer of only one.

1921

The demand for space in the first post-war exhibition was so great, and so many would-be exhibitors were crowded out, that the decision was taken, despite labour unrest and serious threats of a strike, to hold another exhibition in April 1921, only twelve months later.

Political tempers had frayed over the year. In 1920 the RIBA President J. W. Simpson had gone out of his way to praise Dr Addison – 'always courteous, always accessible, and with an unwearying devotion to national housing.' A year later he took a very different tone: 'A fair trial has been

given to the politicians in their adventures into the field of technical competence, and public opinion is fairly unanimous as to their disastrous failure.' (*Bdr* 15 Apr. Suppl. p. i). Simpson was particularly angry with Addison's attempt to speed his public housing programme by 'enforcing drastic measures against all who should venture into what he is pleased to call "luxury" buildings' and he likened this procedure to 'stopping the minute hand of a watch in the hope of thereby accelerating the seconds hand.'

The exhibition maintained the emphasis of the previous year on new methods, especially concrete blocks and slabs, and *in situ* concrete walls. For the first time there was also a major accent on education. Student drawings were exhibited; films were shown; and distinguished lecturers included Beresford Pite and Raymond Unwin.

There was some nostalgia for the old settled Edwardian days. *The Builder* regretted the lack of attention given to developing acceptable surface and textural treatment of new materials like concrete, and looked back to 'those nice pavilions designed by Sir Edwin Lutyens some years ago which so notably revealed his appreciation of external treatment.' At the same time manufacturers should show more care in resisting ornament for its own sake in the design of their stands; consultation with architects 'would be very helpful towards retaining that proportion and restraint in ornament which is still such a crying want,' for 'there is sometimes an over-opulent "profiteer" quality in design which we look to see less of' (*Bdr* 15 Apr. Suppl. p. iii).

The sought-after restraint was shown by S. N. Soole's joinery stand (**24**), designed by E. Bates. This was a simple open pavilion with, at the angles, four attractively worked square piers of deliberately

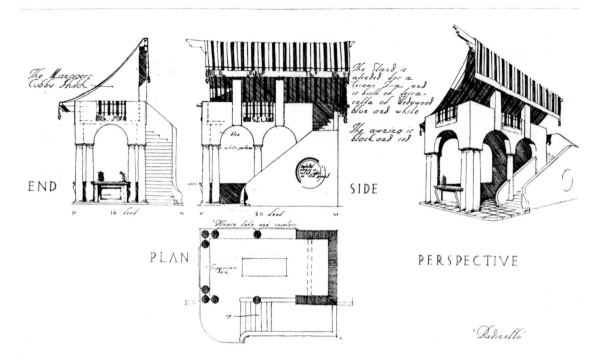

untreated Oregon pine and a fascia with well designed lettering. Similarly controlled were the pair of linked hexagonal brick structures, every face of which showed a different metal window or door, by Crittall (**23**).

1922

The 1922 Exhibition was the third in successive years, and *The Architect*'s correspondent confessed to 'something of a feeling of breathlessness' after the reception, the banquet, the Architectural Association carnival and the dance (until 5 a.m.).

There were two different stand and layout competitions. H. G. Montgomery, who had just been elected an Honorary Associate of the RIBA, sponsored a competition open to students of ateliers affiliated to the Royal Academy, and *The Architects' Journal* a similar one but without restriction to

students. The latter, lamented the assessor, W. G. Newton, President of the AA, attracted only six entries for the layout section, an area certainly calling for attention, for 'the present welter is unduly distressing, and the final impression one long fatigue' (*AJ* 12 Apr. p. 538). This area produced substantially more entries in Montgomery's competition, but layout was to remain a problem and an irritant for many years.

Newton's report on the *AJ* competition distinguished between stands themselves made of the material advertised and those which must provide room for a display of goods. 'Here is need for easy access and yet it mustn't be all access. The patron must be encouraged to linger, and there must be corners for him to linger in. And light must be remembered, and the structure kept simple.' T. F. Rippingham's winning entry (**26**), 'would be remembered. It is suitable for the goods it displays.

There is room to come and go, and room to wait. It carries a simple flavour of Eastern bazaars, and adds a glamour to salesmanship.'

Of the third prize winner ('slightly more outré') he remarked that 'any place where you can sit down is remembered gratefully in an exhibition at Olympia.' Its designer, J. Crowe, also designed a stand at the 1922 exhibition (**25**), that of Building Products Ltd, praised by Frederick Chatterton for its commendable reticence, excellent lettering and harmonious colours.

In general, Chatterton said, the stands are an improvement, though they still fall short of those from before the war, when quite often 'exhibiting firms commissioned architects of the highest repute,' and he deals severely with the modest little brick stand of S. & E. Collier (**27**), which is 'marred by an ungrammatical combination of moulded bricks in the cornice, and other errors which are the hallmark of the amateur designer.'

Harland Paints again showed, as in 1913, a classical composition, columned and pedimented, by Edward Keynes Purchase. The exhibition's most ambitious stand (**28**), however was designed for W. G. Tarrant by J. Sydney Brocklesby: a two-storey half-timbered lodge with an external oak staircase. In its brick-nogged panels were displayed more than thirty different kinds of brick. Work done for current buildings formed a natural source for exhibition. So Crittall displayed, among much else, the new bronze double doors, 14ft by 9ft, for London's County Hall, whilst J. A. King showed the 'Ferro-Glass' extensively used in the same building.

Leckhampton Quarries provided open space with plants and ornaments, and a small gabled and transom-windowed structure. Designed by Leonard Barnard, it was acclaimed as 'one of the most satisfactory in the exhibition' (Chatterton). But 'perhaps the gem' (*Br. Bdr* May, p. 92) was Lionel

29. W. T. Lamb, 1922: Lionel Littlewood. *Br. Bdr.*
30. Bath Artcraft, 1924: C. A. Richter. *AJ.*

Littlewood's red-tiled and handmade brick garden wall and entrance for W. T. Lamb (**29**). Nothing ungrammatical here . . .

1924

1924 saw space problems eased by the opening of the new National Hall at Olympia. The social and political pressures of post-war years however continued to make their impact. The first Labour government was now in office, albeit briefly, and introduced a strong Health Minister in John Wheatley, whose Housing Act, with its long-term commitments, brought about some expansion for the industry. In opening the 1924 exhibition Wheatley took the opportunity to emphasise bluntly that 'his main interest in the building industry was in the provision of working class houses.'

A feature of post-war exhibitions had been the large number of systems of cottage construction, many of them in concrete, but by 1924 these had fallen away to less than a dozen. As a building material concrete retained its dominance, and a welcome development in its treatment was the attention now being given to its aesthetic qualities. As a dithyrambic leader in *The Architects' Journal* (16 Apr.) exclaimed,

and is there not, too, a dawning revolution in Art? How shall the stay-at-homes guess at the new desire for infusing colour into concrete, for bringing proportion and perfection into every form? These things are only slowly to be learned unless we go Exhibition-wards.

Pressure for properly designed stands continued. *The Builder* (18 Apr. p. 638), whilst owning that 'there are still a few pavilions and stalls which are a pleasure to look upon', observed that the more

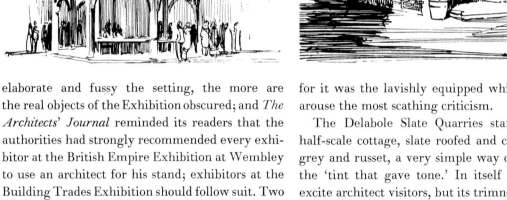

elaborate and fussy the setting, the more are the real objects of the Exhibition obscured; and *The Architects' Journal* reminded its readers that the authorities had strongly recommended every exhibitor at the British Empire Exhibition at Wembley to use an architect for his stand; exhibitors at the Building Trades Exhibition should follow suit. Two months earlier (27 Feb. p. 381), the same journal had run an article 'By A Publicity Expert' on *The Building Trades Exhibition: how to interest the architect.* In it the Expert makes some familiar points. Architects are

essentially men of cultured taste, and the ostentatious will only arouse their prejudice and dislike. The stand must be suitable and effective, and it must conform to principles of good architectural design. Thus it should be entrusted to an architect.

And this course, far from adding appreciably to the cost, would often bring about considerable savings,

for it was the lavishly equipped which tended to arouse the most scathing criticism.

The Delabole Slate Quarries stand showed a half-scale cottage, slate roofed and clad in green, grey and russet, a very simple way of illustrating the 'tint that gave tone.' In itself it would not excite architect visitors, but its trimness is in sharp contrast to the crude and crowded stand of G. Johnson Bros, architectural metal and shop front specialists, which was nonetheless acclaimed in *The British Builder* (May p. 151) as 'one of the brightest stands at the Exhibition.'

A well designed stand which would win the approval of The Expert was that of C. A. Richter for Bath Artcraft's display of furniture (**30**). Quite without ornament except for a painted fret on the wide architraves of the opening, this white pavilion made its effect entirely by its succession of undecorated receding planes. But the most prominent

stand at the exhibition, if not the most widely applauded, was that of Bell's Poilite and Everite, asbestos cement, seen here (**31**) in a sketch by J. D. M. Harvey. From an octagonal base a two-stage tower clad in corrugated sheeting and roofed with pantiles rose to a height of about sixty feet. By exploiting its own airspace it called attention to itself in the simplest and most economical way. S. & E. Collier, reprimanded by *The Architects' Journal* in 1922 for amateurish lack of grammar, this year won its congratulations for a garden house (**32**) designed by A. J. Thomas, who was still designing stands for Collier more than a decade later. If with its powerful barrel-vaulted interior it seems to lack openness and ease of access, we must remember that a brick stand like this is its own exhibit, and that the figures shown in Harvey's sketch are peering not into the interior but at the wall textures themselves.

The promoters' wish to set the Exhibition in a context wider than simply that of building technology showed itself in 1924 in a special display of architectural draughtsmanship. Seen as a deliberate counter to the many current exhibitions of architectural work which were illustrated by photographs, this display had an impressive rollcall of contributors including Baillie Scott, Dawber, Goodhart-Rendel, Herbert Baker, Oliver Hill, Maufe and Ernest Newton.

1926

By 1926 the Conservatives were back in office. At the opening of the exhibition Sir Kingsley Wood, Parliamentary Secretary to the Minister of Health, spoke solely of housing. Since the war 602,724 houses had been built, two-thirds of them private, and he quoted the last year's record – 159,026, of which 126,936 had been built by private enterprise. After expressing his doubt of the government's capacity to continue this achievement if there was to be 'a great industrial stoppage' (the General Strike began five days after the close of the exhibition), and making only glancing reference to the need to tackle slum clearance 'much more vigorously than we have been able to up to the present,' he particularly hailed the fact that the house-building programme of the previous year had included more than 25,000 houses built by new methods, particularly in steel and in concrete.

Music had returned to the Exhibition. *The Architects' Journal* (14 Apr. p. 575), whilst admitting how much it had enjoyed the band and the air of bright and brisk prosperity, grumbled on about the bewilderment and nervous exhaustion brought about by the lack of system in the layout. At the same time it asserted that a

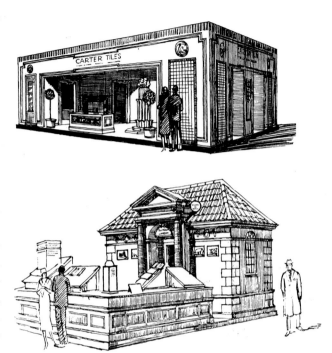

building exhibition is probably the most useful of all exhibitions . . . It is of enormous practical value to a professional architect, but to a layman it may be an intellectual revelation. And it is a revelation which may be obtained in a single afternoon.

The promoters organised a prize essay competition for 'My Impressions of the Building Exhibition 1926', to be judged by the PRIBA, Guy Dawber, the President of the AA, H. S. Goodhart-Rendel, and the President of the Architecture Club, J. C. Square (*sic*) an unhappy misprint for Sir Jack Squire, poet, man of letters and founder of the Architecture Club. A consolation prize went to the architect and critic F. E. Towndrow, who in the 1930s was to take into partnership the distinguished German refugee Eugen Kaufmann, thus enabling him to practise in this country. But the winner was H. G. M. Waters, whose essay reasonably enough bore out *The Architects' Journal*'s claims. As a

'wondering youth,' he says, he passed from sprightliness to leg-weariness, but in the process he acquired 'a liberal education.'

In *The Architect & Building News* (16 Apr. pp. 353–4) an architect cast his mind back. Despite honourable exceptions, and he singled out Crittall, earlier shows were 'in a measure "thrown together" and formed in the aggregate a most unattractive (almost repellent) display' whereas now 'well designed and ordered stands are almost the rule.' But although he commended upwards of a dozen stands he mentioned (perhaps knew the names of) no designers. He awarded the palm to Atlas White Cement (33), recently used as a proofer in construction work at Liberty's, Dickens and Jones and Selfridges. The display was a striking concept for its date, showing different surface treatments of white stucco cement linked by three plain sawn beams finished in blue; 'both substance and manner of presentation touch the highest level of direct simplicity.'

Carter and Co. of Poole created some interest with their simple rectangular pavilion (34), at once restrained and inviting. Another admired stand (35) was that designed by Welch and Hollis for Langley London to display roofing tiles and interlocking pantiles. This showed the way it should be done instead of what *The Architect & Building News* called 'the bad old habit of pitchforking a miscellaneous collection of goods onto a counter.' As in 1922 Lionel Littlewood was the architect for W. T. Lamb's stand. Seen here in surroundings distinctly more idyllic than those provided by Olympia (37), this was a but and ben cottage displaying different kinds of brick and tile properly and harmoniously used and showing (said *The Builder*) 'how the need for small buildings can be met without disfiguring the countryside' (9 Apr. p. 633).

1928

No post-war government had been allowed to forget about 'Homes fit for heroes', and in 1928 the race to get houses built was still on, to the detriment of the crafts side of the industry. What used to be called substitute materials had now become standard and were much in evidence – asbestos-cement tiles, building blocks, cast stone.

The long-running debate over the Exhibition's layout continued, and *The Builder* changed sides, accepting, despite its earlier doubts, that the present method was the best. Neither exhibitors nor visitors favoured grouping, and dispersal 'obviates any possible embarrassment.' Moreover, exhibitors liked to retain a regular position. The same journal welcomed the large number of stands now designed by architects, for the best way of displaying a product, it said, is in a building of real architectural quality (*Bdr* 6 Apr. p. 586).

There were fewer complaints about the importunities of hucksters on the stands. The shift of promotional emphasis was illustrated in an ironic comment in *Building* (May p. 202) that there were 'so many special samples, handed out with such generosity, that after a few visits the proceeds could be made over to someone to assemble a house for nothing.'

Since the earliest days both the journals and the promoters themselves had deliberately broadened the trade fair basis of the Exhibition by mounting regular displays of architectural drawings. This year the promoters carried the idea further with a major Architects' Loan Exhibition of *objets d'art*, with 160 items on show, some of considerable splendour. Unfortunately no catalogue of the exhibits has survived.

Walter Tapper, PRIBA and chairman of the exhibition, himself designed the stand for the Gas

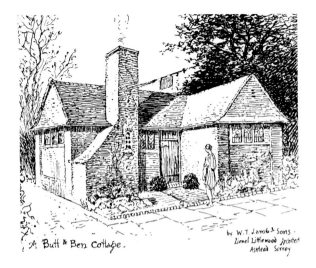

A Butt & Ben Cottage.

by W.T. Lamb & Sons.
Lionel Littlewood Architect
Ashtead Surrey

Light and Coke Co. (**39**), a suave, substantial and fully furnished pavilion with an open loggia. His predecessor as President nearly thirty years earlier, Sir Aston Webb, also had a stand in the exhibition. Following the death of Lionel Littlewood, whose stands had brought them much favourable comment over the decade, the brick firm W. T. Lamb had turned to Webb, or to his practice since he himself was now 79 years old, to design for them a woodland shelter with a steep conical roof supported on piers which form four bays of different kinds of bricks and four columns of spiral brickwork (**36**).

The Atlas White stand departed radically from the successful simplicity of 1926, going instead for the display of part of a 'real' building under construction, as Crittall had shown details from Whiteleys in 1911 and the LCC's County Hall in 1922. The Atlas display included a replica of the base of one of the Egyptian columns from the Carreras factory in Camden Town, by M. E. and O. H. Collins. Later in the year the young modernist architect Maxwell Fry wrote an assessment of the building for *The Architects' Journal*. He criticised it as a sententious sham in its heavy Egyptian mode (which referred to the Black Cat symbol of the cigarette brand), but with characteristic honesty owned that it was nonetheless 'rather beautiful' (*AJ* 21 Dec.).

The exhibition marked the first appearance of a leading 'modern' architect in Joseph Emberton, who designed a stand for Thames Board Mills (**40**), a largely unadorned structure which simply proclaimed its purpose and invited further enquiries. Emberton, best known as the architect of Simpson's shop in Piccadilly (1935–6), was starting work at the time of the 1928 exhibition on the New Empire Hall at Olympia, which would help to house successive exhibitions for another forty-five years.

Venesta showed a trimly designed modern rectangular box (**38**), very different from what was to

39. Gas Light and Coke Co., 1928: Walter Tapper. *Bdr.*
40. Thames Board Mills, 1928: Joseph Emberton.
A&BN.

come at the next exhibition, and there were other slight stirrings from the winds of modernism elsewhere at Olympia. The journals continued to vie with one another over their own stands (usually illustrated only in their own pages). The Architectural Press, soon to be the great champion of the Modern Movement, commissioned the traditionalist Professor A. E. Richardson (later to be architect-President of the Royal Academy) for their stand, whilst *The Architect & Building News* went to Adshead and Ramsay. Here (**41**), through a distinctly Mussolini/Italianate frontage an open atrium is entered between two sets of three undecorated columns, each enclosing diagonally-set rectangular sheets of glazing. The impact of the Moderne, of the 1925 Paris Arts Deco Exposition, had arrived at Olympia.

Modernism Arrives

1930

In 1930 the Exhibition, with its four hundred exhibitors, was switched for the first time to late September, where it was to remain throughout the thirties, until it moved, from 1947 onwards, to the end of November. Labour were now in power, and the exhibition was opened by Viscount Burnham, who, in contrast to Sir Kingsley Wood four years earlier, reported that 243,500 houses had been built in Greater London in the past ten years; 'he was glad to say that 45% of that total was due not to private enterprise but to public benevolence' (*Bdr* 19 Sept. p. 484).

Chief amongst the great range of stands was the revolutionary and absolutely assured Venesta stand by Le Corbusier and Charlotte Perriand. Venesta had been exhibiting regularly for more than twenty years. Their stands were always elegant and clean-cut, and 1928 had brought their Twenties-modern shell. But in the following year Jack Pritchard, who had joined Venesta in 1925, became familiar with Le Corbusier's work in Paris and, encouraged by the design publicist John Gloag who worked for the advertising agency holding the Venesta account, he got Le Corbusier to design the 1930 stand, his first and only work in Britain.

Birch plywood frames divided the space diagonally, plywood on one side, Plymax (armoured plywood) on the other. The polished aluminium Plymax ceiling was supported by two stanchions, of plywood and Plymax, by a birch tree trunk and by a vertical tube from which pivoted leaves of Plymax and a Plymax door. Spot-lights shone alternately up to the ceiling and down to the exhibit, and the diagonal of the layout was bisected by a full length roof-height hanging sign proclaiming the name of the company. The axonometric drawing (frontispiece) shows the stand with the ceiling removed, the photograph (**42**) the stand as completed.

Bryce White's stand came from a totally different world. As many of the firm's products as possible were lumped together into a jostling ensemble, and the result looked unlikely (to speak temperately) to have had the attention of an architect. Somewhere between the two came a display of traditional joinery which, apart from its absence of cluttering furniture, might have appeared at any of the century's exhibitions. This was the Jacobean hall and staircase (**43**) for John Sadd & Sons, designed by George Coles and worlds removed from the super cinemas, like the Gaumont State at Kilburn and the Trocadero, Elephant and Castle, for which its designer is remembered today.

Another stand untypical of its architect was the Sika stand (**44**) by Berry Webber, the town hall specialist. Here he is in a very different mood, producing a light-hearted pavilion closer to the British Empire Exhibition at Wembley in 1924 than to the Paris Arts Deco Exposition of the following year. But it is not just a *jeu d'esprit*. It demonstrates the principle that to draw the crowds (as the Sika stand did, and as Pilkington did by having their armour-plated glass assaulted by steel hammers) there is no better way than to have something *happen*.

Within the glass case were two walls, one leaking water from a number of tiny holes, the other with a one-inch jet of water squirting from it; and oil-skinned workmen were regularly and rapidly sealing them both.

Another stand which caught the interest of visitors was the Silent House, designed by Trystan Edwards. This comprised a number of rooms en suite. Ten firms, including Venesta, Crittall, Troughton & Young and London Brick, collaborated in the whole. Each room was designed and decorated by Edwards (one of them was painted by Christopher Jacobs, son of the novelist W. W. Jacobs), and each contained a compartment where visitors might carry out their own sound-proofing tests.

It was not only in its stands that the 1930 exhibition showed its range. It brought within its scope, probably for the first time, the wider environment. So the Cement Marketing Board had a display of Colorcrete, pink and buff concrete designed to brighten up the drabness of our road surfaces; and the Council for the Preservation of Rural England had a stand reflecting the serious and growing concern over the despoiling of landscape, showing good and bad examples of building development, advertisements and petrol stations. The stand was all part of the CPRE's lively campaign for preserving the environment which ran through the inter-war years, master-minded by the architect of Portmeirion, Clough Williams-Ellis.

1932

By 1932 Banister Fletcher's Presidency had given place to that of Raymond Unwin, the National Government had replaced Labour and the exhibition was opened by W. Ormsby-Gore, First Commissioner of Works.

Well over a decade had passed since the end of the war with its high hopes and high promises, and disenchantment had set in. Many people felt that complacency and evasiveness were now the order of the day; jerry building was rife; and a world slump was under way. Battle lines were drawn up between the traditionalists, determined to preserve or restore the spacious standards of pre-war days, and the young modernists, in full cry in their determination not to let what they saw as the old gang's entrenched smugness make a mess of things all over again. But the industry was reluctant to embark on the new methods and untested materials demanded by impatient young architects, an understandable enough view and one often justified in the event.

Some of these new materials found their way to the exhibition, where wider national concerns were also reflected in a remarkable display organised for the London (Voluntary) Housing Societies by Elizabeth Denby, the galvanic housing consultant who later worked closely with Maxwell Fry on pioneer working-class housing projects like Kensal House in Ladbroke Grove and Sassoon House in Peckham. Called *New Homes for Old*, it displayed good and bad planning at various levels, town, village, house. Besides a specially designed model flat (by Mrs J. C. Shepherd and Miss Janet Fletcher) and illustrations of German working-class housing, there was also a shock section on slums, with horrifying pictures and pinned-out specimens of rats, beetles and other vermin.

This fierce prodding of the national conscience coincided with the worst of the Depression. In February 1932 32.8 per cent of all unemployed were drawn from the building industry, and at the exhibition H. G. Montgomery organised a raffle of donated books and drawings together with a gala dance at Olympia, which together raised 1,000 guineas for the Architects' Unemployment Relief Fund. And the RIBA, with the London Society, mounted an exhibition of maps, plans and measured drawings which had been made under the Architects' Employment Scheme. In other ways too the economic depression outside could not be altogether escaped within Olympia. Close to a visionary model of London Airport, to be constructed on the roof of King's Cross Station, was a display of vegetable garden produce mounted by the Society of Friends. A surprising item perhaps to find at a Building Exhibition, its intention was to encourage the cultivation of allotments by the industry's unemployed, as a means both of providing a useful activity in itself and of keeping fit until the slump was over.

But the exhibition as a whole was determinedly bright and forward-looking. It had a larger number of well-designed stands than ever before, with work across the architectural spectrum from Walter Tapper and Edward Maufe to Emberton and Wells Coates (whose first appearance this was) and new young partnerships like Yorke and Gibberd. HMS *Endelline* was still afloat, though destined for mothballing after the close of the exhibition. At the same time another familiar symbol was making its first appearance in Marley's Oasthouse, which, whatever the changes in the main body of Marley's stands, was to form an unaltering trademark backcloth for nearly forty years.

But visitors alert to the design of stands must have taken away with them an overriding impression of the new modern (and Moderne). Emberton did at least three stands, for Samuel Williams Cast Stone, for ICI and for Williams & Williams, this last (46) an ingenious juxtaposition of eighteen different types of Reliance windows and screens in a single composition which lay invitingly open without revealing all at first glance. After their success with Le Corbusier in 1930 Venesta put the design of their stand to Wells Coates. Again

Jack Pritchard was the instigator. Pritchard had recently set up his own company, Isokon, for the unit design of houses, flats, furniture and fittings with Coates as architect/designer. Coates was already working for Pritchard in Lawn Road Flats in Hampstead, a block which was to be one of the notable achievements of the Modern Movement in Britain. For Venesta at Olympia he designed a long low stand (45) of telling simplicity to display the flexible and decorative qualities of plywood. The entire stand was made of the product it so effectively advertised.

The year also marked the first appearance of Raymond Myerscough-Walker, better known for his fine and idiosyncratic draughtsmanship. He designed two linked stands for Masonite (grainless woodboard) and Lacotile (wall linings). The Lacotile stand, seen here (47) in Myerscough-Walker's characteristic sketch, was designed to show how

readily this material could be cut to any shape. Was the bar as openly hospitable as the illustration suggests?

Middle-of-the-road work was shown in the London Brick Co. and Forders stand (48) by Julian Leathart, architect of Whitgift School and of Dreamland at Margate. Here standard bricks, none specially cut, were used in great variety to show the wide choice of texture and colour available, and their versatility was further demonstrated by their use to form a 6ft. 6in. flat arch span without reinforcement. Leathart, who became London Brick's regular designer, always included in his stands one virtuoso element like this. On the traditional front Wheatly & Co. had an open pavilion (49) which displayed their flooring tiles, a new building tile for the columns, hexagonal tiles for the turret base and some ingenious tile hanging for the turret itself. The designer was Edward

46. Williams & Williams, 1932: Joseph Emberton. *AJ.*
47. Lacotile, 1932: Raymond Myerscough-Walker. *AJ.*

48. London Brick Co. and Forders, 1932: Julian Leathart. *AJ*.

1932–1934

Maufe, work on whose competition-winning design for Guildford Cathedral was already starting, and behind his agreeable composition lay a display which must have warmed the heart of the sales manager.

But it was the modernists who dominated. Manufacturers were more ready to use untested designers and untested methods in exhibition stands than they would have been in the erection of permanent buildings, and Olympia 1932 was a good shop window for the new architecture, supported by the press. *The Architects' Journal* for instance carried an article by Baird Dennison on colour in architecture. Dennison was in fact a pen name of P. Morton Shand, oenologist and leading publicist for contemporary architecture, and behind his apparently simple plea for a more imaginative use of the possibilities inherent in coloured materials lay a coded message to architects to look beyond their

own shores to France, Germany and Sweden, to see how to design in (and not just to employ) coloured concrete and glass. One of the few stands he mentions by name is Carter's eminently Twenties stand (**50**) by Stanley Hall and Easton and Robertson, who had designed the British Pavilion at the 1925 Paris Exposition and were to do the same at the New York World's Fair in 1939. Their brightly coloured stand showed the decorative possibilities of Carter's tiles, faience, terrazzo and pottery.

1934

At the 1934 exhibition, opened by Lord Balfour, Sir Giles Gilbert Scott the PRIBA touched on an issue which had been echoing down the years when he said in his introduction that he looked first to see if the layout allowed easy circulation, second at the

designs of individual stands, and last at the exhibits themselves. Battle lines had been drawn before the war. Professor Richardson had returned to the attack in 1921, calling not for regimentation but for a logical plan which would lead the spectator through a series of impressions in sequence. Montgomery riposted that it would be almost as difficult to impose a universal scheme of house building and when the matter was raised again in 1930 he totally rejected 'the extraordinary views' of some architects over the design of the Exhibition. 'With unfailing regularity', he wrote in *The Builder* (12 Sept. 30 p. 435), 'each year produces some genius' who proposes cutting up spaces into circles and squares and rectangles. But this, he said, would exclude ninety per cent of the present exhibitors. Firms had pegged out their particular spaces for many years and it would be useless to offer them uniformity of space or design. No doubt an excellent

idea for a chocolate exhibition or a fashion fair, it would be utterly impracticable for the infinite variety of building accessories. The matter swelled into a major dispute in the pages of *The Architects' Journal* in 1934, with many distinguished contributors, not all on the same side – Myerscough-Walker and Skinner of Tecton for instance in complete opposition to each other. But the organisers remained adamant, no doubt to the relief of regular exhibitors; and the exhibition attracted 120,000 visitors in a fortnight.

Following the success of the London Housing Societies' 1932 display the Housing Centre organised another *New Homes for Old* exhibition, centring this time on an analysis of slum clearance problems in Bethnal Green by the MARS Group, the sole embattled association which provided a platform and a forum for modern architects and their sympathisers. The leading figure in the analy-

50. Carter, 1932: Stanley Hall and Easton and
Robertson. *AJ*.
51. Venesta, 1934: R. T. F. Skinner of Tecton.
RIBA: BAL.

52 *Architectural Design*, 1934: Towndrow and
Kaufmann. *AD.*
53. *The Architect & Building News*, 1934: Noel
Musgrave. *A&BN.*

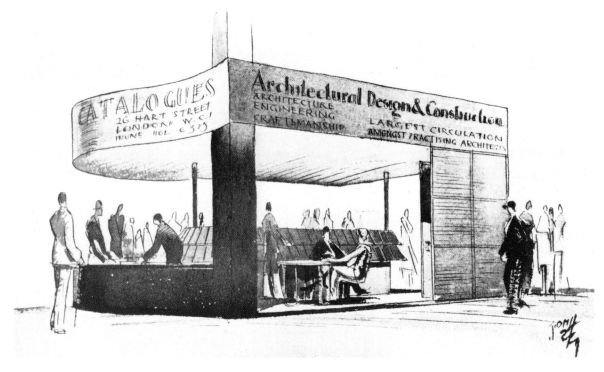

sis was Wells Coates, and he continued to work on
the problem until in 1937 with the private developer Randal Bell he found a site in Bethnal Green
where skilfully planned modern housing could
transform living conditions and at the same time
yield an economic return. Despite the strong social
awareness of so many avant-garde architects, this
scheme was one of the few opportunities which
came their way to apply their skills to working-
class housing. But the war killed it.

A section devoted to Planning the Small Flat
showed three contrasting designs: by Louis de
Soissons for the Duchy of Cornwall's Kennington
Estate, by Emberton for the Chapman Estate, and
the '1935 Flat' by Sir Aston Webb's practice, to be
built within the shadow of Westminster Abbey.
Fig. 56 shows a not very informative glimpse of the
latter seen from the Architectural Press stand, designed by F. R. S. Yorke. The space and openness

of his design for the Press were in marked contrast
to the unwelcoming stand beyond for George M.
Callender.

After their stands by Le Corbusier and Wells
Coates in 1930 and 1932, Venesta organised an
open competition for stand design in 1934, very
probably the first which resulted in a stand being
actually built. The winner was R. T. F. Skinner of
Tecton. This practice had been formed in 1930
when a group of young graduates from the Architectural Association invited the Russian Berthold
Lubetkin, who was working in Paris, to join them
in England. Tecton created a stir with the Penguin
Pool and Elephant House at the London Zoo, and
under Lubetkin's brilliant leadership they went on
to produce some of the decade's finest work, including the Finsbury Health Centre and the two High-
point blocks of flats in Highbury. Skinner adopted
Lubetkin's proposal to use a natural birch trunk

for the support of floating freeform plywood bands overhead, a light-hearted counterpoint to the rectangular plywood screens displaying the product and showing photographs of executed works, along with all the other prize-giving designs for the stand, by Jack Howe, Gordon Cullen and others (**51**). All was plywood, the stand itself, the frames, the exhibits, the bent plywood seats, and the result (said *The Architects' Journal*, 20 September), was 'an absolute joy; never has plywood looked so very like itself, even on the stand designed by Le Corbusier for the same firm.'

A salesman on the stand was the young Paul Reilly, son of Sir Charles Reilly, Head of the Liverpool School of Architecture. Now a director of the Building Trades Exhibition, Reilly was to become an influential figure in the promotion of good design. In 1978 he was created a life peer.

It did not escape criticism. Julian Leathart, him-self a regular stand designer from the Thirties to the Fifties, claimed it as capturing 'that gloriously care-free spirit which so speedily evaporates at the end of an architect's student days,' but the prosaic truth was that parts of it were slung by steel wires from the hall's roof. He congratulated the designers for extricating themselves from 'the awkward pre-dicament' presented by 'the meandering lid, which showed signs of distress before the Exhibition opened', and complained that the stand's lack of solidity meant that because one could see through it from almost all angles it had no point of focus.

By this time all the leading journals were backing their criticisms of ill-designed stands ('a prominent and awful example by a tile firm', said one of them about a 1934 stand, 'which embodies nearly every possible fault') by taking space themselves. Illustra-ted here is Towndrow and Kaufmann's stand for *Architectural Design* (**52**), in a sketch by J. D. M.

57. Frederick Braby, 1934: Verner O. Rees. *Bdg*.
58. British Steelwork Association, 1934: Sir John Burnet, Tait & Lorne. *Bdg*.

Harvey; Myerscough-Walker's sketch of *The Architect & Building News* stand (**53**) by the young Noel Musgrave, then on the paper's staff and later to be a distinguished editor of the *RIBA Journal*; Myerscough-Walker's own fantasy of a stand (**54**) for *The National Builder*; the open and elegantly curved plywood stand (**56**) by F. R. S. Yorke for the Architectural Press, incorporating a blown-up photograph of Lubetkin's Penguin Pool at the London Zoo; and Julian Leathart's design (**55**) for *Building*. Only *The Builder* let the side and itself down with a plain box untouched by imagination. Between them these six stands suggest something of the range of architectural design in the mid-Thirties; it was not all neo-Georgian, mock-Tudor, zigzags and little white cubes.

A small mystery attached itself to Leathart's *Building* stand. Prominent in his drawing of it is a huge photograph of the newly opened headquarters of the RIBA, designed by Grey Wornum. As executed however, a last minute substitution replaced Wornum's building with another of the year's showpieces, Giles Gilbert Scott's Cambridge University Library. Could this have been in compliment to Scott, PRIBA and the chairman of the 1934 exhibition?

Wornum himself was responsible for a neat little stand for George Jennings of Lambeth, the chief interest of which lay in an ingenious space-saving bath designed by Wornum for the small flat. This was another indication of the increasing importance of small flats as a design type, reflecting something of a shift in living patterns, which had already emerged in the flat-planning section of the *New Homes for Old* display.

The Sussex Brick Co. had an austere rectangular brick pavilion by their regular designer Verner O. Rees (who had just won the competition for the library at the University College of Swansea and was to be President of the AA in 1938) in place of

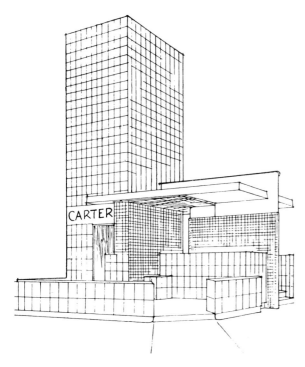

what Leathart called their 'dreadful prehistoric mammal' of 1932. Rees was responsible also for a small and applauded house (**57**) for Frederick Braby. This was a compact little anthology of what were popularly regarded as the main superficial motifs, the gestures, of British modernism – the horizontal windows, the semi-circular glazed frontage, the sun terrace, the white exterior with external stair. But unlike its kin springing up across the home counties it was an all-steel house with the main skeleton plaster-rendered over dovetailed sheeting and every detail of the interior down to the stairs and the picture rails carried out in Braby's metal products.

A more remarkable steel structure was the stand (**58**) designed for the British Steelwork Association by Sir John Burnet, Tait & Lorne. Its very largely glazed upper floor was cantilevered out from six internal piers encased in standard unit steel sheet-

ing to form a hollow central trunk which contained a steel staircase. Painted royal blue with two horizontal bands of vermilion and white knife-edge lettering, it was an early example of those quintessential Building Exhibition stands of the next two decades, adventurous, assured, with a touch of swagger about their daring which hinted at the sophisticated near-magic that met you as you crossed into Olympia from the humdrum streets outside.

1934 saw the first of Kenneth Cheesman's series of designs for Pilkington's demonstrating the structural and decorative use of glass. Mrs Darcy Braddell did graceful kitchen stands for Vono and Electrolux, Sir Walter Tapper again designed the Gas Light and Coke's exhibit, Oscar Bayne did a boldly 'moderne' stand for A. Johnson & Co. (London), demonstrating their Savestain steel for kitchen units, and F. R. S. Yorke did three stands in

61. London Brick Company, 1936: Julian Leathart. *AJ.*
62. Architectural Press, 1936: F. R. S. Yorke and
Marcel Breuer. *AJ.*

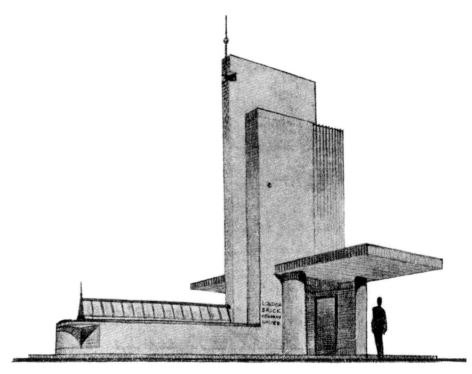

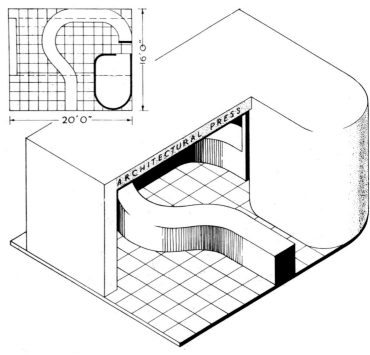

63. Milton Hall Brick, 1936: J. E. Newberry. *A&BN*.
64. S. & E. Collier, 1936: A. J. Thomas. *A&BN*.

1934–1936

all. Uganda joined other Empire countries for the first time, and government research stations – Building Research, Forest Products, National Physical Laboratory – were much in evidence.

1936

The 1936 exhibition, opened by Earl Stanhope, First Commissioner of Works, included another outstanding Housing Centre display of planning, nursery schools, and clinics under the title *Britain is Being Rebuilt*. The organisers were Judith Ledeboer and Elizabeth Denby with help from the MARS Group and the socialist Architects' & Technicians' Organisation (ATO), whose Honorary Secretary was Skinner of Tecton, and the layout and setting were in the hands of Misha Black. King Edward VIII paid an informal visit to the exhibition, one of the very few public engagements of his short reign, and spent most of his time at the Housing Centre display. Already in 1934 at the RIBA's centenary celebrations he had come out as a forthright advocate of mass production in tackling the problem of the Distressed Areas, and this display caught his special attention.

The Architects' Journal (17 Sept. p. 361) commented on the extraordinary diversity of the exhibits, where glass bricks rubbed shoulders, as it were, with twisted wrought iron knockers. It was possible, it said, to find all the material necessary to build a fine house of four hundred years ago, and almost exactly in the same form; it was equally possible to build a house entirely from materials on display which had been unknown before the war.

This diversity was naturally reflected in the range of stand design; from Samuel Elliott's Tudor panelled room and the frisky little Gothic edifice (**63**) for Milton Hall Brick by J. E. Newberry and Fowler, through A. J. Thomas's humble pavilion

(**64**) for S. & E. Collier – he had been designing their stands for twelve years – to Oscar Bayne's stand (**59**) for Carter's of Poole, a series of vertical planes for displaying tiles, comprising the four faces of a tall vertical tower with lesser planes for smaller tiles abutting it and projecting over a covered terrace.

Modernism certainly did not sweep the board. But it predominated amongst the more striking stands, whether in the work of the true pioneers like F. R. S. Yorke or in the many stands which were simply gesturing light-heartedly with the attractive if superficial motifs of the avant-garde.

After their successes with Le Corbusier, Wells Coates and Tecton, Venesta turned naturally enough to a distinguished furniture designer, R. D. Russell, for their stand this year. The Architectural Press used Yorke and the refugee Bauhaus architect Marcel Breuer, whom Yorke had recently taken into partnership to enable him to practise in this country. Built in gloss-painted plywood, their simple and authoritative stand (**62**) had a serpentine central counter with bright blue flanks leading back into an enclosed office. The floor was white lino, all lettering was in red.

Julian Leathart again took the opportunity to show the versatility of brick in his stand for the London Brick Co. In 1932 he had spanned a wide flat arch with unreinforced brick; now (**61**) he cantilevered two five foot long projecting hoods from his main brick structure by using ordinary bricks with the reinforcement laid in the mortar joints. This caused some comment: *The Architect & Building News* frostily called it a permissible joke in an exhibition stand but not one to be embodied elsewhere by young enthusiasts (18 Sept. p. 353); a case of the biter bit in view of Leathart's own lofty mockery about the 1934 Venesta stand.

A demonstration of the allures of the modern manner was to be seen in the contrast between the

1934 and the 1936 stands of the Cement Marketing Company, both designed by Henry Tanner. The pedestrian no-nonsense pavilion of 1934 (**65**) gave way at the later exhibition to a lightweight open stand (**66**) with fashionably glazed flank, set on the slope, and a 32ft pylon.

1936 was the first year in which Ascot Gas Water Heaters exhibited, and appropriately for a firm with a sharp concern for the quality of design in all its products it put the design of its stand (**67**) out to competition. The winner was Rodney Thomas, a founder of the Arcon practice in 1943 which was to establish an admired and emulated exhibition design style. Ascot returned to Thomas and to Arcon for its stands over nearly twenty years.

Thames Board Mills put their design (**60**) to a commercial firm of exhibition designers, John Edgington, who produced for them one of a series of variations on a highly idiosyncratic theme which they had begun for Treetex at the previous exhibition. They were ingenious and powerful visual trademarks, modern in treatment, inescapable in their prominence, somewhat lacking in hospitable welcome to the visitor.

1938

Outside, the world moved inexorably towards war. Hitler's troops marched into the Rhineland in March. The Abyssinian war ended in May. The Spanish Civil War wore on. The next Building Exhibition opened in the middle of the Munich crisis in September. Indeed it was on the closing day of the exhibition that Chamberlain flew to see Hitler at Munich, returning next morning with his message 'Peace with honour. I believe it is peace for our time.'

68. James Clark, 1938: Raymond McGrath. *RIBA*: *BAL*.

The tensions of the time account for the unusual happenings at H. G. Montgomery's lunch at Olympia, where the high spot, according to *Building* (Oct. p. 430) was the impromptu singing of God Save The King. 'Only the builders sang with any real abandon and gusto. The architects, except for Mr Culpin, sang thinly, with evident and characteristic embarrassment,' leaving the writer to reflect that 'it is the MARS Group and not the Building Trades Federation that I expect to meet behind the barricades.'

A luckily unrealised nightmare which haunted the promoters during the final run up to opening was the fear that general mobilisation would be announced. Most of the exhibitors and their staff would vanish overnight; Olympia itself would very likely be commandeered; and there would be little or no labour force to dismantle the half-built stands and to strip out the entire hall.

As it turned out, 'with the world staggering through the worst international crisis since the Great War,' commented The *Architect & Building News* (23 Sept. p. 352), 'the prosperous bustle and sublime normality of the Building Exhibition seem something of a miracle . . . The only reminder that the world was not its old delightful nineteen-twentyish self' came from the pervasive presence of air raid precautions. A bomb-proof casualty station was on display; Sealocrete water-proofer made much of its ability to keep out mustard gas; similar claims were made by the Limmer & Trinidad Lake Asphalt Company and by Hope's windows; and the British Steelwork Association's stand concentrated on the application of structural steel against blast.

Pilkington, foiled in their efforts to move their celebrated glass train into Olympia, had three stands, all designed by Kenneth Cheesman. One

dealt with double glazing and sound insulation. The second, a remarkable V-shaped stand, largely transparent, displayed their new toughened Armourlight glass (again with telling stress on air raid resistance). The third, a house of glass, had a wall of glass bricks supporting the firm's name in slender neon lights. Inside were every kind of glass and a staircase with armoured glass treads leading up to the gallery.

A different approach to glass display came from the architect Raymond McGrath, specialist in the use of glass, in his stand (**68**) for James Clark, who had made all the glass for McGrath's design for Mansfield Forbes's celebrated house 'Finella' at Cambridge. Here all was light, open and fanciful, but precisely calculated to the various uses of glass and its facing onto flat and curved surfaces. The stand was sited in a part of Olympia dominated by machinery and heavy brick structures, and it effec-

tively called attention to itself not only by sheer contrast but also by the use of water running down a fluted glass chute wrapped round a 20ft Vitroflex tower and splashing into a pool at the base lined with glass tiles. The drawing shown here is McGrath's own design, from the RIBA's Drawings Collection.

Rodney Thomas, who had won Ascot's stand competition in 1936, again designed their stand, or rather two stands linked by overlapping free-form roofs over a public walkway. Metal rods from floor to ceiling created an impression of enclosure without losing the feeling of spaciousness. All plumbing was exposed by being carried through a synthetic glass screen instead of being concealed behind a solid wall, and sink heaters poured a continuous stream of hot water into a trough.

Julian Leathart had been commissioned by the promoters to supervise the overall design of the

exhibition, a post he was to hold until 1961, when he was succeeded by Michael Wolstenholme. Among the displays by 440 exhibitors at least forty stands were designed by architects, of many stylistic persuasions, including Maxwell Fry, Bertram Carter, Gerald Lacoste, Oliver Bernard (who took over the stand design for Colt Shingles from Emberton and for the Cement Marketing Company from Tanner), and Vincent Harris the town hall architect. Oscar Bayne again did Carter's stand, and Leathart again did the stands for *Building* and for London Brick; the special feature of the latter was a 60ft reinforced brickwork beam.

Maxwell Fry's stand (**69**) was for Hunziker's, displaying their Uxbridge Flint Bricks. The bricks were in blue, brown and grey pastel shades, some of which Fry had used in his design two years previously for the Gas Light and Coke Company's notable working-class housing at Kensal House,

Ladbroke Grove. The claim to special strength made for the bricks was supported by the fact that Swiss Federal Railways had entirely rebuilt the second Simplon tunnel with them. Fry followed Yorke's lead in his Architectural Press stand of 1934 by winding a blown-up photograph round the curving wall of the office. Thirties architects well knew the thrilling impact of modern photography as pioneered in the *Architectural Review*.

Much else went on in addition to the trade stands. Building research was served by a series of displays by DSIR (the Department of Scientific and Industrial Research), exploring twenty-seven separately identified and immediate problems, from dampness and smoky chimneys to wind pressure and rendered finishes. Many of the Schools of Building, among them the Northern Polytechnic, Kingston, Brixton and Hammersmith, had displays of student work, and on the social front the organisers con-

71. Rural Housing exhibition, 1938: cottage by Justin Blanco White. *AP*.

1938

tinued their tradition of defraying the costs of the hall, the band and the food for an Architects' Benevolent Society ball, with all proceeds to the ABS.

Finally there were the exhibitions within the exhibition. Whitbread's sponsored a show of modern public house design, decorated by paintings from the year's RA Summer Exhibition by Munnings, T. C. Dugdale and Algernon Talmadge. The MARS Group reassembled, and tailored to the space available, their New Burlington Galleries exhibition of the previous January. Designed to show the relationship between modern architecture and the twentieth-century way of life, it had an entirely recast planning section, the fruit of their radical Plan for London: a huge East-West spine with ribs North and South of graded units, neighbourhood, borough and district.

The Unit Flat exhibition showed a flat 'ideal for

bachelors of either sex', said the publicity, comprising the Entertaining Room, the Bedroom, the Cocktail Pantry (designed to give the butler, or perhaps the host, ample elbow room), the Kitchen and the Radio Study, sound-proofed since few town dwellers 'have not been troubled by the wireless nuisance.' G. E. W. Crowe was the organising architect, Walter Goodesmith designed the Radio Study, and among the designers of its Easiwork furniture were Ernö Goldfinger and Raymond McGrath.

The theme of the *New Homes for Old* exhibition, now a regular feature and organised by Judith Ledeboer, was Rural Housing. Its centrepiece was a five room cottage designed by Justin Blanco White, displayed alongside an authentic rural slum house (**70, 71**). The latter had been occupied until a fortnight before the exhibition opened, when it was dismantled, transported and re-erected at

Olympia. The organisers also bravely brought to London its rustic occupant. No doubt to widespread relief he was heard to express a preference for the new cottage, though a writer in *The Architect & Building News* wistfully hankered after taking over the old place as a weekend retreat.

Brave New Post-War World

1947

The 1947 exhibition opened in a different world from that of its predecessors. Opened by Charles Key, Minister of Works, it took place at a time when the balance of payments crisis had just brought about drastic reductions in the capital investments programme. The Blitz had massively and impartially destroyed good housing stock and bad; at the same time there was an acute shortage of almost every material, and an equal shortage of skilled workers. Restrictions, controls, were everywhere. Observers remarked on the notable lack of domestic heating appliances on show, and many exhibitors in all fields, familiar from pre-war days, stayed away, unwilling to seek orders they would not be allowed to fulfil. The emphasis on goods for export could be seen not only in the product field but also in building plant, where about thirty firms, most of them newcomers to Olympia, were displaying a great variety of plant which, said *Architectural Design*, 'we should like to see grinding and chugging away on our own building sites, now perforce abandoned to the willow-herb, the ragwort and the sallow.'

The industry's innovative capacity had not however stood still over the previous eight years. It had been tested from Mulberry Harbour to prefabricated houses, and work of the first importance had taken place in the application of standardisation to component design. DSIR had published the Housing Manual and the Post-War Building Study series,

and the biggest exhibitor in the entire exhibition was the Building Research Station. Lightweight cranes and tower hoists, all manner of new materials and applications for structural work and finishes, were to be seen at Olympia and, tantalising though it was to gaze through the shop window at the unattainable, 162,399 people thought it worth doing so. They also had a glimpse of what would soon become commonplace: the English Joinery Manufacturers Association stand, which was designed by Frederick MacManus, showed designs for a double-glazed casement. Double-glazing, commented *The Builder*, is rarely seen in this country (though Pilkington had been making it, and displaying it at the Exhibition, in the 1930s).

As always there was a full programme of exhibitions. *Europe Renewed*, on post-war reconstruction, had contributions from a number of overseas governments, including those of Belgium, Holland, Czechoslovakia and Poland. *This Was London* showed pre-war drawings of buildings now destroyed. The Council of Industrial Design showed three typical furnished living rooms, and the London Brewers' Council pointed the way to better pubs. Finally Mrs Darcy Braddell and Lawrence Wright designed an entertaining *Back Yards* exhibition, contrasting 1910 (complete with housewife's bloomers on the line, an old tyre hanging from a tree branch and fish bones picked clean by the cat) with a supernaturally spotless mockup of the same area as the LCC envisaged it for 1950.

There was no great abundance of architectural work for practices struggling to start up again after

72 (*previous page*). The 1947 exhibition at Olympia: general view. *AP*.
73. James Clark and Eaton, 1947: Cecil Handisyde. *AP*.

the war or for the new generation of architects fresh from the forces. Among the forty-four designers known to have contributed stands to the 1947 exhibition were many later to become familiar figures, Brian O'Rorke, Keith Murray, Hulme Chadwick for example. And a number of young practices were making what must have been among their earliest appearances: Lyons and Israel, Eric Brown and Stefan Buzas, Kenneth Bayes of the fledgling Design Research Unit, and Anthony Cox of the Architects' Co-Partnership, whose stand for Boulton & Paul showed that the 'Festival of Britain' style four years hence was a culmination, not a new beginning.

Richard Nickson and Sir Patrick Abercrombie did the London Brick stand, at much the same time as they were working on their post-war town plans for Bournemouth and Warwick. The specialist designer Richard Levin did stands for Warerite and

for Cellon, for the latter of which he had already designed their 1938 exhibit, and the Aluminium Development Association went for their cantilevered tubular scaffolding stand to the sculptor Lynn Chadwick. Trained as an architectural draughtsman, he worked with Rodney Thomas immediately after the war, increasingly concentrating on sculpture – he had three works at the South Bank Festival of Britain – and achieving international recognition with his competition-winning *Unknown Political Prisoner* of 1953.

Cecil Handisyde designed the stand (**73**) for the glassmakers James Clark and Eaton to show the many practical applications of glass possible even in times of restricted supplies; the port-holed walls of the office at the right of the illustration were constructed entirely of hollow glass blocks. Handisyde, who had already designed a stand in 1938, was to complete at least ten more in the 1950s, mainly for

74. Thomas French and Sons, 1947: Wells Coates. *AP*
75. De La Rue Gas Development, 1947: Deryck
Vesper. *AP*.

1947

the National Federation of Clay Industries and the
National Coal Board.

The stand (**74**) for Thomas French and Sons was
designed by Wells Coates, by now a Royal Designer
for Industry. The exploded perspective illustrated
here shows his way of achieving the display of a
large number of small items, metal 'fixits' for
attaching cladding, curtain rail fittings, webbing
for Venetian blinds, and the like. The open stand
contained a number of sculptural objects, each displaying aspects of the firm's products: the salesman's desk on the left, for instance, was surrounded by a shaped screen of linked curtain rings,
suspended from a rail which showed French's special curtain tape, whilst the Y-shaped supports at the
back carried sections of dummy wall and window
displaying curtain rail fittings.

A stand which created a great deal of preliminary
interest was the result of a competition organised
by *Art and Industry* and sponsored by De La Rue
Gas Development. The conditions called for quality,
attractiveness and a working display of gas water
heaters, cookers and fridges, with full provision for
circulation and access for demonstration. From the
87 entries received the judges (L. H. Hardern, PRO
for the Gas Light and Coke Co., Grey Wornum and
Leigh Ashton, Director of the Victoria and Albert
Museum) chose the design by Deryck Vesper (**75**).
As executed however, the stand aroused little press
comment, partly perhaps because it was erected in
a corner at Olympia where it could not be seen to
full advantage.

The designers who made the most impact were
the young practice of Arcon, which showed during
its fairly brief existence a remarkable talent for
display work. Formed in 1943 as a partnership of
Rodney Thomas, A. M. Gear, Edric Neal and
Raglan Squire, they were responsible for no less
than five stands in 1947, for B. Finch and Co., Celotex, ICI, Ascot Water Heaters and Williams &

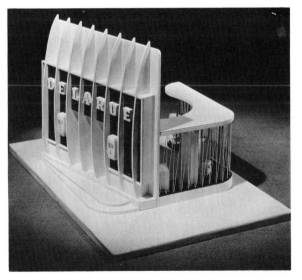

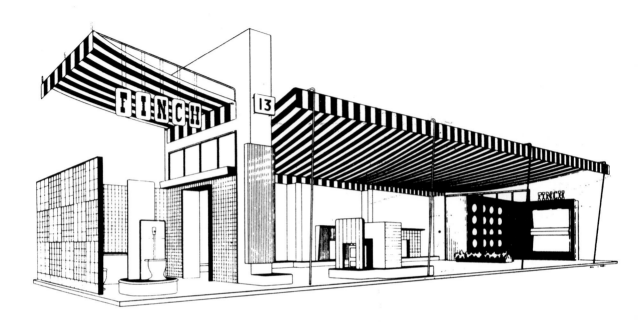

Williams.

The Finch stand (**76**), drawn here by Andrew Bain, who was to be the witty and resourceful designer of the Brick Development Association stands in the 1970s, tackled the problem of creating a unified display of their diverse products, heating and cooking equipment, fireplaces, bathroom and lavatory fittings. The designers made use of an obdurate buttress of the hall structure to divide the stand into two main sections, of sanitary fittings and fireplaces. The existing flue services of the back wall were utilised for a working fireplace display; an island site showed a complete heating system in cutaway sections; and the decorative striped awning both screened off the overhanging gallery roof and acted as reflector for the concealed lighting.

Williams & Williams had a two-level stand (**77**). Ground floor comprised reception and an aluminium window display. The cantilevered staircase

(with aluminium treads, like the escape staircase) led to an upper terrace which showed an inclined Aluminex roof glazing system as a canopy; this was canted at an angle which allowed easy inspection, and was supported by a tubular steel mast, the thrust of which was rooted in a load-spreading timber base at ground level, itself concealed by a heather garden bed.

The designs for Ascot and for Celotex showed a similar fresh approach, whilst the difficulty of displaying how the great range of ICI products contributed to the various stages of building was solved by the adoption of a circular layout. Standard free-standing panels, which did not need to be viewed in sequence, were grouped round a central umbrella feature which not only gave scale but also cut off the immense height of Olympia's roof, a hazard for any open-topped stand. The circular pattern allowed access from any direction, and the

more permanent display items, casement windows, kitchen equipment and the like, were grouped in and around an office and at the edge of the stand.

1949

In 1949 the exhibition was again held under the shadow of capital investment cuts. Aneurin Bevan, Minister of Works, opened it with a well-informed speech which, against the odds, had his audience under its spell. He made two points of substance, in commenting on the failure so far to devise a constructional system which did not unnecessarily restrict or bully the architect, and in stressing his determination to resist any importunings to lower housing standards by substituting quantity for quality.

The 415 exhibitors showed between them a full range of technical developments, and they looked forward, in confidence or in hope, to a future unshackled by economic privations. As always however the exhibition had a wider context as well, exemplified in 1949 by special displays on Shopfronts Old and New, Wallpaper through the Ages, Antique Joinery Tools, and a stand by the Georgian Group setting out its achievements and its aims.

There was press comment that stands were becoming simpler, in a welcome reversal of the trend typified by the 1946 Britain Can Make It exhibition where the display was sometimes so elaborate as to swamp the exhibits themselves. Writing of the 1949 exhibition, a severe critic in *The Architect & Building News* (9 Dec. p. 601) remarked that 'exhibitions of this sort are not primarily held so that architects may walk round in a transport of delight as they congratulate each other and themselves on the outstanding merits of the design of

their stands.' Of course, he says, you do better to use a competent designer, but you must avoid over-organisation. He was much taken, he professed, with the view from the gallery at Olympia, 'reminiscent of a fairground grafted on to the old city of Jerusalem by night.'

The most novel stand (**79**), one still spoken of with a certain intake of breath by those involved in the 1949 exhibition, certainly did not exemplify any movement towards simplicity. Designed for Lafarge Aluminous Cement, it was the work of James Holland, one of the most imaginative of specialist designers, and Peter Chamberlin, partner in the dominant post-war practice of Chamberlin Powell and Bon. Cantilevered from a single pillar, far off centre, and approached by twin staircases suspended from tubular handrails, its platform slab had a maximum depth of 6½ inches, tapering to 3 inches at the edge. An incidental benefit of this

design where all the action took place at the first floor level was the consequent lack of ground level bulk and the creation of much needed free floor space. The stand was cast and prestressed, using the Freyssinet system, in six days on the site. Despite exacting prototype testing, its daring and innovative character led the exhibition organisers to insist on their own tests before they would allow the public up the stairs, and twenty large men were employed to jump in unison on the end of the cantilever, without mishap. The stand was set in a 4ft foundation block below floor level with a reinforced concrete base slab. After the exhibition the demolition of these foundations presented such problems that the remains are said to be still there. No doubt they will puzzle a future generation of industrial archaeologists.

Another unusual stand (**78**), drawn here by Donald Dewar-Mills, and asking the enquiring

visitor to crane his neck, was the sinuous tile-sweep designed for Carter's by John Lacey of Playne and Lacey, who had succeeded to the practice of Sir Aston Webb. All the tiles displayed, plain, morocco-faced, ribbed, grooved and pinhead were in buff to concentrate attention on their textures. In contrast, and showing the importance of paying attention to floor coverings, was the floor pattern, where circles of alternating dark green and black were laid centrally on light green or yellow terrazzo blocks. The stand did not meet with universal admiration, one journal sharply characterising it as 'a very extraordinary display of what can be done with tiles if you try hard enough.'

Despite its brooding overhang, a stand could hardly be more open than was Carter's. At the opposite pole was the display called Design for Recreation devised by Kenneth Lindy for a wide range of collaborative sponsors including the Nat-

ional Trust, the Youth Hostels Association, the Boy Scouts and the Girl Guides, the RAC, four architectural schools and a number of major manufacturers like London Brick, ICI, Pilkington and Crittall. Its entrance was built out over Olympia's gallery walkway so as to be clearly visible from the main hall downstairs, and it had no need to buttonhole the visitor's attention with a single range of products; but did the carefully unfolding of the plan induce a feeling of overcrowding or of being too enclosed?

Among other notable stands were those for *Building* by Oliver Hill, that most fashionable architect of the inter-war years, for the Zinc Development Association by Stefan Buzas and Fello Atkinson, for Merchant Adventurers by Paul Boissevain, for James Clark and Eaton by Wells Coates, and for Ruberoid by Eric Brown and Peter Chamberlin (again). Of new young practices Stillman and Eastwick-Field did the stand for the

Eastwood Brick Group, and Edward Mills that for Twisteel Reinforcement. ICI's stand was by the specialist designer Beverley Pick, who was to design most of the finest Christmas decorations for London's Regent Street; members of the Design Research Unit (DRU) did stands for the Cement Marketing Board, the Fire Protection Association and Berger's Paints; and Crittall's stand was the outcome of a competition held in the Liverpool School of Architecture and won by F. Rogerson, whose subsequent career was to be spent in Dublin.

Arcon were again responsible for Williams & Williams's stand, and Rodney Thomas himself did a stand for Ascot, which was much more modest than their previous displays. It came in for some harsh criticism, one commentator saying that 'in place of the really slap-up and imaginative they have contented themselves with a few naked fluorescent tubes and some various sized concrete blocks which leave their demonstrators standing about looking like dispossessed penguins.' Nor did the RIBA escape criticism. Its stand and club room, said *The Architects' Journal*, were 'embarrassingly lacking in taste. Please, RIBA, with all these clever builders and engineers looking on, show some design ability.'

Two names later to win distinction in the public authority field did stands: for Neuchatel Asphalte, Whitfield Lewis, the LCC's Principal Housing Architect in the 1950s before becoming County Architect of Middlesex; and for the Timber Development Association Roger Walters, TDA staff architect at the time, and later to be Chief Architect to the GLC. His was an elegant and unassertive stand (**80**) of four parabolic arches with cantilevered tabletops for display. With no sense of crowding it found room for models of recent timber houses, models and drawings to illustrate design sheets on timber trusses for industry and commerce, a display of glued laminates, samples of tropical timbers which could be imported without licence – and room too for visitors to move about it.

1951

By 1951 the long run of the post-war Labour government had come to an end. At the exhibition's opening in November David Eccles, Minister of Works in the new Conservative administration, asserted that the government had inherited a half-bankrupt economy which demanded a temporary cutback in starting rates for all works except houses, where the target was to be an ambitious 300,000 a year. The government intended to relax controls and to give the industry the long-term conditions to expand. This message of hope was welcomed, and the exhibition itself suggested some optimism; certainly this was the first time it had filled not only the Grand Hall and the National Hall but also the ground floor of the Empire Hall.

Among the special features were the history and work of stonemasonry, in a display organised by Lawrence Wright, and the Village Joiner's Shop, both of them underlining the need to re-establish the traditional crafts; and a show of contemporary architectural drawings, including Basil Spence's prize-winning designs for Coventry Cathedral.

Some of the best stands, like the Ministry of Housing and Local Government's *New Towns – New Ways of Life*, came from government departments, research stations and the nationalised industries. The latter, like Cecil Handisyde's stand for the NCB, constructed like so many others by City Display, took their place among the commercial stands, but the government displays, usually designed by unnamed official architects, maintained the strongly didactic note characteristic of the immediate post-war years.

About fifty stands are known to have been the

work of named architects and designers. Among them were now established exhibition designers like Leathart, Arcon, Kenneth Bayes of the Design Research Unit, Richard Levin, and Eric Brown and Peter Chamberlin, with a two-storey tubular stand for Ruberoid. Newcomers included Robin Day for ICI, John R. Harris with the first of his long series of stands for London Brick, Douglas Stephen for the Expanded Metal Company, and Noel Moffet with a dapper little stand for Twisteel.

The towering design event of the year was the Festival of Britain Exhibition on London's South Bank. It is hard now to recapture the lift to the nation's spirits this gave. Almost all the leading younger designers shared in a collaborative celebration of what could be done were it not for the brooding austerity which the country had endured for a decade. The Festival did not create a new style, though it provided a useful and much used stylistic label. With its blond laminated wood, its tubular frames, its running of outside and inside into one, its indoor plants and its landscaping, with 'architectural' lettering and decoration everywhere, it was an exhilarating potpourri of an international design style which was in fact nearing its end. Lightweight design seemed to imply much sought after lightheartedness, and its design significance was that it established for the ordinary public, by means of a dazzling fête, an appropriate Welfare State architecture. Here were the jolly colours, the 'balls-and-string' motifs, the splayed and spindly-legged chairs on which the espresso coffee generation would soon be sitting. Here were the shining and all too imitable sources of the increasingly gimcrack work which was to clutter the High Street stores over the next twenty years. And many a stand at the Building Exhibition, in 1951 and in previous years, could have been shipped unnoticed from the South Bank.

The stands of the glass and window companies

83. Carter, 1951: Yorke, Rosenberg and Mardall. *A&BN.*

84. Eastwood Group, 1951: Stillman and Eastwick-Field. *A&BN* (?).

formed an interesting group at Olympia. Besides Arcon's stand for Williams & Williams and S. E. Ware's for Henry Hope, there was a striking tubular scaffold for Chance Glass by Paul Boissevain, with a set of prototype figured glass designs (by Sadie Speight, wife of Leslie Martin of Festival Hall fame, among others) put out 'on approval' for exhibition visitors. After the long run of designs by Kenneth Cheesman, Pilkington used their new house architect S. M. Sternfeldt to produce a festive 'Alice Through the Looking Glass' theme (**81**). Glass panels illustrated scenes from the book, and the central feature, supported on a light steel frame, was Alice's crown made from different types of figured glass. Everything on the stand was glass: steps, floor, balustrades, door, table.

Wells Coates again did the stand (**82**) for James Clark and Eaton, with new transparent ventilating units in glass brick panels and a 'reference library' of 150 glass samples. The central features of this notably uncrowded stand were two glass polyhedra, each of five cubes intersecting in the ratio of the Golden Section, though not every visitor spotted their scholarly basis.

Crittall meanwhile had held a competition at the Architectural Association School for their stand. It had been won by four students calling themselves Group E (Peter Matthews, Michael Cain, Bob Maguire and Michael Brawne). Their highly praised stand, a spaceframe, showed windows, ventilators, sun-breakers for hot climates, and on the first floor a large screen of standard fixed lights coupled together and left unglazed and unpainted to show the etched hot dip galvanised finish as it left the factory for installation. There was plenty of space on their stand and a marked absence of those lengthy and all too rarely read explanatory captions.

Carter's of Poole (**83**) went this year to F. R. S. Yorke's newly established partnership of Yorke, Rosenberg and Mardall. With special floors of

marble and terrazzo, their main theme was Carter's new hand-painted tiling, and a series of walls showed glazed tiles hand-painted by Peggy Angus, which YRM were already using in a new primary school on the Lansbury Festival site in Poplar. The job architect was Neville Conder, who later in the decade was to design a number of Crittall stands with Michael Cain (of Group E) before entering into partnership with Hugh Casson.

The Eastwood Group stand (**84**), by Stillman and Eastwick-Field, had a ground floor made up of the Group's manufacturing products: bricks, cement, curb units, aggregates and a window opening made from a section of a giant sewage pipe. Alongside the coloured facing brick staircase was a tree symbolising the company's growth since 1815, whilst the exterior of the first floor was faced in new permanent colour-burnt weather tiling.

The Zinc Development Association had a crisp display, designed by Stefan Buzas, then of James Cubitt and Partners, and later to join with Alan Irvine to form a highly distinguished exhibition practice. His sculptural stand (**85**) had a showcase for smaller hardware of zinc and zinc-protected items, and as its main feature a tripod of galvanised steel scaffolding from which small areas of zinc roofing, laid in differing systems, were suspended.

1953

H. C. (Stow) Montgomery had died at the end of the war, and H. G. (Greville) Montgomery retired at much the same time, so that the organization of post-war exhibitions was in the hands of H.G.'s son Hugh and his wife Molly. Three days after the close of the 1951 exhibition H.G. died, followed two months later by Hugh. Henceforth, and for

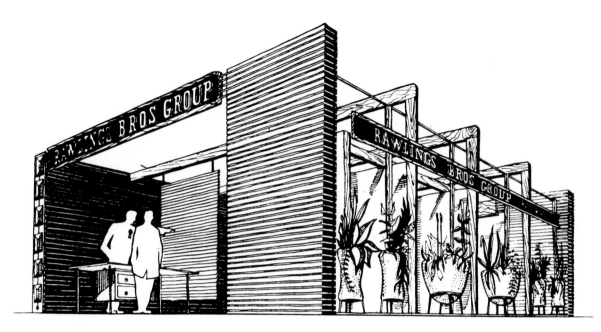

well over thirty years now, the exhibitions have been headed by Mrs Molly Montgomery and her son Bryan (H. B. G. Montgomery).

1953 was Coronation Year. It also saw the Silver Jubilee of the Building Exhibition, the twenty-fifth exhibition since 1895 and still inexorably growing. With nearly six hundred exhibitors, the organisers took over the first floor of the Empire Hall for the first time. Opened by Harold Macmillan as Minister of Housing, it took place in an atmosphere of some optimism and promise of prosperity. The Minister spoke of 'the new housing crusade' and tried to re-enlist the 'moral factor . . . the sense of a great national purpose', which had galvanised the country during the war years.

Timber had just been freed from controls (though it still had to be paid for out of foreign exchange) and the government was trying to make inroads into the other side of the housing problem by mounting Operation Rescue on slum clearance and by what soon came to be called rehabilitation.

So, among the special exhibitions, the MOHLG's *New Life for Our Towns* put a special stress on saving older houses by improvement and conversion, calling attention to the grants available under the Housing Act 1949. Another major special exhibit was very different. The Ministry of Fuel, the nationalised authorities, the research associations and private industry combined to present a display of the Heat Pump, already in use in the Royal Festival Hall, which promised great fuel economies by taking the unwanted heat from the surrounding atmosphere and adding it to the building's air and water supply.

There was one other collaborative special display, that of the Prestressed Concrete Development Group, co-ordinated by the Cement & Concrete Association. The group, which included contractors,

engineers, architects, product manufacturers and equipment suppliers, was an important demonstration of the Building Exhibition's role in promoting innovation. A continuous display of pre-stressing beams on the spot drew the crowds, as any activity and movement always do amongst otherwise static exhibits. In 1949, when prestressed concrete made its first appearance at the Exhibition, there were only thirty prestressed jobs in Britain. By 1953 there were over a thousand, evidence of its profound importance in modern building. The display called attention also to its export potential, not least by illustrating the Tampa Bay Bridge in Florida, fifteen miles long, with a $3\frac{1}{2}$ mile section in prestressed concrete designed and manufactured in Britain.

The overall level of the stands was high enough by now for a waggish columnist in *The Architects' Journal* to suggest that quality had reached a point where it was perhaps possible 'to contemplate photographing those stands which stand out because they are so appallingly *bad.*'

The Eastwood Group went again, as they had done since 1949 and were to do until 1957, to Stillman and Eastwick-Field, who produced a finely detailed stand in the black-painted steel frame tradition. Chance Glass turned to H. T. Cadbury-Brown for a stand designed to suggest ideas for the home, the office and the shop. Within his display, which had an exterior wall clad in painted glass and a glass mosaic screen, were full-size mock-ups of kitchen, bathroom, living room and office, where the living room for instance was equipped with shelves, cupboard doors, coffee table top and fireplace surround – all in glass.

The Sussex and Dorking Brick Company, who had used Verner O. Rees as their designer since 1934, went this year to the old-established practice

of Lanchester and Lodge. The outcome, in sharp contrast to the firm's customary work, showed a winding wall of coloured prefabricated brick panels inset in dark brown brick frames mounted in an exposed cream tubular framework. The tables were of brickwork and the curved office wall screen was of octagonal tiles.

'First' stands from young architects came from Roderick Ham and Guy Sheppard for Chaseside Engineering, an ingenious and flexible prefabricated stand on a 3ft module, designed for re-use at subsequent exhibitions; and from Cassidy, Farrington and Dennys for Cape Asbestos. Both these practices had been formed by recently graduated Architectural Association students. Younger still was R. H. Gordon, a second year student who had won a competition at the Hammersmith School of Building sponsored by Rawlings Bros and assessed by Wells Coates. His assured stand (**86**) centred on

the firm's work in rebuilding and repair; its designer was to go on to the AA, graduating in 1958.

Philip Dowson, who had graduated from the AA that summer, was already embarking on his association with Ove Arup which was to bring him the Royal Gold Medal for Architecture in 1981. With Francis Pym he designed an elegantly cool stand (**87**) for C.D. Productions showing Arup's Punt roof system which was already in use in two of the notable schools in Hertfordshire's pioneering programme. The sculpture was by Oliffe Richmond, an Australian who came to England just after the war and worked with Henry Moore. He was to die sadly young.

Another youthful practice, Ryder and Yates, working for the Gotham Company, manufacturers of Carlite Plaster, produced a stand (**88**) which already showed the strongly sculptural forms that were to be a feature of their award-winning

buildings in the north-west over the next thirty years. The architects published an account of the background to this their first stand design in *Northern Architect* (no. 4, May 1962, pp. 65–69): '. . . Practically the only job in the office, it created a great deal of excitement. It was as if we had been asked to design a cathedral.' The client wanted a strong presentation of too many products, and this would inevitably entail

a solution which would disappear into the bric-a-brac of Olympia. To convince a client that to get one idea across in terms of building and display is an achievement, and that the rest of the story should be left to their representatives on the stand, was, and always seems to be, the most difficult design task to accomplish.

Ryder and Yates go on to indicate the difference between stand design and other construction jobs; months to design and days to build, and at the con-

struction stage the need to be on site night and day. 'Lack of sleep helps to create a terrible sense of frustration' and, echoing Cecil Handisyde's judgement that stand design is 'a pleasant nightmare', they 'question the sanity of the decision to accept such a commission.' The arrival of the directors, alert and bowler-hatted, at nine a.m. 'increases the torture of the occasion' but 'come ten o'clock, magically all is complete.'

The Design Research Unit was again to the fore, this time with a lightweight stand (89) of rectangular planar surfaces for D. Anderson of Stretford. The horizontals showed examples of built-up roofing systems, a full-size aluminium decking system was suspended over the office area, whilst the verticals contained roofing felts and a relieving patterned wall. The prominent Red Hand was the trademark of the company. Design was by John Diamond with Misha Black as consultant, whilst mural decoration and typography were by Jock Kinneir.

The Design Research Unit was a new and highly influential kind of multi-disciplinary grouping which ranged right across the field from architecture and industrial design to graphics and packaging. The DRU had been founded in 1943, with Herbert Read as its first manager. Founder members included Milner Gray (head of the exhibition design department of the Ministry of Information), Misha Black and Kenneth Bayes, and among its associates were Frederick Gibberd, Sadie Speight, Robert Gutmann and the engineer Felix Samuely. The Unit's development was the earliest indication of the shift in exhibition work away from the architect as stand designer towards the graphic designer and later towards the display artist working within shell stands and the emergence of the advertising agent as a major power.

1955–1971

Squeeze and Boom

1955

The next exhibition, in 1955, was opened by Nigel Birch, Minister of Works, and enlivened by the visit of a large body of Russian building technicians.

Great interest was aroused by the model layout of a redesigned Soho for the year 2000 by the Pilkington-commissioned Glass Age Development Committee (comprising G. A. Jellicoe the landscape architect, Edward Mills the architect and Ove Arup the engineer). But the dominant special theme of the exhibition was to be found on twenty or more stands devoted to aspects of timber as a modern building material. Here were sections on rigid frame construction, on the work of specialist groups like the Society for the Protection of Ancient Buildings (SPAB), the Forest Products Research Laboratory and the Men of the Trees, photographic displays of outstanding modern timber buildings, and stands from France, British Columbia, the Gold Coast, Nigeria and North Borneo.

The specialised building products company Tretol, whose own stand, along with a dozen others, was designed by the exhibition firm Olympia Ltd, sponsored a competition for a House for the Professional Man, to cost no more than £4,250. There were 323 entrants, Clifford Culpin was the assessor, and the winning design, by R. Towning Hill & Partners, received a distinctly unenthusiastic press. Many exhibitors went again to designers they had used before, among them Williams & Williams (Yorke, Rosenberg and Mardall), British Plaster-

board (Ronald Dickens), the Eastwood Group (Stillman and Eastwick-Field), Ruberoid (another eye-catching display by Eric Brown), Cement Marketing Board (Kenneth Bayes of the DRU), London Brick (John R. Harris) and Stramit Boards for another elegant and unobtrusive stand by June Park.

There was little that was novel on display, and with so many manufacturers content to offer variations on their existing themes the technical press showed some disgruntlement with stand designers. It was agreed that government stands were unimaginative and dull (though they were to recover effectively at the next exhibition). More generally, *The Builder* (25 Nov. p. 979) thought many stands over-elaborate. It was

a point of honour to have a stand which is architecturally well designed, but one cannot help feeling that this is sometimes given too much consideration to the detriment of the main purpose of the stand, which is to show what the manufacturer has to offer.

The Architect and Building News (24 Nov. p. 656) complained of monotony:

Two storeys being popular and curves virtually out, we have a mass of cubes and boxes, more or less framed up, in wood or in metal but mostly in wood.

The feeling of disenchantment emerged still more strongly in *The Architects' Journal* (24 Nov. p. 691), whose columnist

tires of the clever stuff and turns with relief to the simple and the straightforward. Exhibition architecture

91. Ascot Gas Water Heaters, 1955: Dennis Pugh. *AP*.
92. Architectural Press, 1955: Dewar-Mills Associates. *AP*.

has had a very good run for the last ten years. It is time it took, or was given, a back seat.

There was however much to interest the visitor on the stands apart from the products themselves. John Pinckheard's Lead Development Association stand, for instance, contained an unexpected pleasure: Epstein's model for his Madonna and Child destined for the linking bridge between the pair of Palladian houses in Cavendish Square. The Chance Glass display, by Lady Casson, was designed to show how glass could bring colour and life into the home, the shop and the restaurant by the use of transparent screens, coloured light fittings and light-reflecting wall surfaces. As well as the work of Royal College of Art students she showed a mosaic glass panel by Humphrey Spender built up of unevenly-set one-inch squares of different glass.

Ascot again put their stand to competition, attracting 160 entries, including a 'refreshingly stark stand' by Alison and Peter Smithson, winners of the landmark Hunstanton School competition four years earlier. The Ascot competition was won by Dennis Pugh of the Architects' Co-Partnership. His surprisingly spacious steel-framed stand (**91**) was consciously muted, in black, white and blue, to mark it out from what its designer expected would be the hubbub of its neighbours at the Exhibition.

Another highly regarded stand was Neville Conder and Michael Cain's for Crittall, built up of the firm's less well-known products, including aluminium double-hung sliding sashes, louvres, screens, sunbreakers and, as its central feature, a sample of the purpose-built windows being installed in the Royal Palace in Baghdad.

Gordon Cullen's stand (**90**) for the Carter Group was instantly attractive, showing the imaginative use of glossy and matt wall tiles, external and internal, in the different settings of factory, home and pub, all deployed in unmistakable Cullen patterns.

93. Gotham Company, 1957: Ryder and Yates.
J. G. Ryder.
94. Gas Council Engineering Research Station,
Killingworth, 1968: Ryder and Yates. *RIBA: BAL.*

Cullen, a major contributor to the eminence of the
Architectural Review, put his stamp also on the
Architectural Press's own stand (**92**), the first of
many to be designed by Dewar-Mills Associates,
with a photographic blow-up back wall screen of
the Press's early-eighteenth-century premises in
Queen Anne's Gate:

1957

It was now fifty years since the Exhibition was first
held at Olympia. Henry Brooke, Minister of Housing, was unable to arouse any great enthusiasm in
his opening speech. Building had flourished in the
last few years, but the high bank rate and other
forms of credit squeeze were making it impossible
for the industry to meet its costs, and cutbacks in
the volume of work were clearly on the way. Indeed, before the exhibition had run its course, the
government announced severe reductions in capital
investment. The particular value of the exhibition
in the circumstances was in pointing the way to
means of stepping up productivity and efficiency.

There were special shows from British Rail and
from the Historic Churches Preservation Trust (designed by Dennis Lennon), which had come on
from that now forgotten venue of stimulating small
exhibitions, the concourse of Charing Cross (now
Embankment) underground station. But the most
notable was *Clean and Decent*, a history of the
British bathroom and w c, organised by Lawrence
Wright, which became a hugely successful book. It
was of course a great deal of fun; the setpiece of
Victorian bathnight beside the kitchen fire, and a
heroic display of lavatory basins and seats, especially
from royal trains (including one of 1847, memor-
ably padded and quilted), drew gasps of admiration.
But it was also a serious precursor to the more
recent attention architectural historians have given

95. Atlas Lighting, 1957: John and Sylvia Reid. *AP*.
96. Adamsez, 1957: Dewar-Mills Associates. *AP*.

to how, as well as where, people lived.

A strikingly original approach to stand design came from British Plaster Board's designer Ronald Dickens. No clamorous lettering, or clever screens to obscure the product (and the customers from the manufacturers' representative): simply a modestly raised open and accessible platform with a tree and, hovering overhead, a trademark hawk as the sole vertical features. Ascot again used Dennis Pugh, who had won their competition in 1955, as they had previously gone again to Rodney Thomas, winner of their 1936 competition. Stillman and Eastwick-Field again did the stand for Eastwood, this time incorporating part of the Gallery overhead with displays at four levels, and their gift for finely-detailed, open design in which nothing was allowed to get in the way of the best possible display of their clients' products brought them the commission for another fine stand, this time for Concrete Ltd. The Gotham Co. (Carlite) were by now firmly established with Ryder and Yates, who produced a sophisticated and economical stand (**93**) comprising three elements, a long and graceful desk, a tall inverted cone and, at the back, a lofted cube, some 15ft square, set on the slant, and minimally decorated with graphics, all sitting on a floor of multicoloured silk-screened felt. The practice's award-winning Gas Council Engineering Research Station at Killingworth, 1968 (**94**) shows the continuity of their design approach.

Dewar-Mills Associates not only did the Architectural Press stand again, but also those for the Plastic Marketing Company, Durasteel and Adamsez. This last (**96**), an aptly clean and decent display, was a more complex layout than the illustration suggests, with well-designed floor patterns and changes of level. Its special features were its huge (but not overbearing) A–Z lettering and its consistent use of vivid red and black to set off the whiteness of the wares.

Newcomers to the Exhibition were the husband and wife team of John and Sylvia Reid, architects specialising in industrial design. Their open modular stand (95) for Atlas Lighting used the product both to light the display and to form patterned elements in the design.

Such integral use of the product was of course at the heart of the brick stands. John R. Harris's stand (97) for London Brick used panels big enough to show how the bricks really looked in use, but overall the stand seems overdressed and restless; every inch, the very stanchions themselves, calling and competing for attention. In contrast Cecil Handisyde's National Federation of Clay Industries stand (98) offered the visitor time and space to compare and to ponder with an absolute minimum of publicity graphics.

A writer in *The Architect & Building News*, approving Cassidy, Farrington and Dennys' stand for Cape Building Products (whose stand they did from 1953 to 1965), characterized its style as 'humanized new brutalism. Less humanized', he added, 'is Theo Crosby's stand for the Architects' Standard Catalogue, which is, however, gayer than his last effort.' But it was quite deliberately a basic structure. Using prefabricated timber for walls and stairs, it was put together in one day, after which the verticals were painted white and the horizontals black. Lettering was minimal but absolutely clear. Crosby plainly thought that an exhibition stand with a fortnight's life was no place for refined and costly finesse. Given his skill as a designer his stand's obvious impression of being knocked up produced a contrast, arguably to its clear advantage, with the elaborately finished stands all round it. Crosby, who was technical editor of *Architectural Design*, owned by the Standard Catalogue Company, was to be the co-ordinating architect of the

98. National Federation of Clay Industries, 1957:
Cecil Handisyde. *AP*.
99. Carter Group, 1959: Nigel Lewis. *AP*.

1957–1959

memorable International Union of Architects site
buildings south of Charing Cross railway bridge on
London's South Bank in 1961, and the leading
spirit in the design consortium of Pentagram.

1959

In his speech at the opening of the 1959 exhibition
Lord John Hope, Minister of Works, was able to
point out that the industry's output had markedly
increased and that costs had remained stable since
the last exhibition. But to overcome shortages he
called for flexibility in specifying, which gave rise
to some head-shaking.

Commentators at the exhibition found fewer
new ideas and products than usual, though a good
deal was so described, and they characterised the
show as one of consolidation. They agreed also on
the high level of stand design. Black and white and
natural timbers were now the fashion, and so many
stands impressed a critic in *The Architect & Building News* that to make his display stand out from
its neighbours the really daring manufacturer, he
suggested, 'will now furnish it with an aspidistra,
two leather armchairs, a box of samples and a
cuspidor.' As at every exhibition there were nonetheless some stands which it is a kindness not to
illustrate, though only rarely are the originators of
their designs known.

Two stands were the result of competitions organised by manufacturers. For Sussex & Dorking
United Brick W. H. Saunders and Son designed
a near-cube of brick sample panels held on a light
steel frame of black tubing, the offices, with photo-
mural friezes, being up the staircase within the
cube. The Carter Group winner was Nigel Lewis
with a Miesian frame (**99**), steel verticals and timber

100. *The Builder*, 1959: Stillman and Eastwick-Field. *John Stillman.*
101. Adamsez, 1959: Dewar-Mills Associates. *AP.*

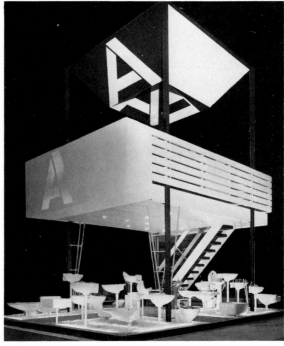

horizontals, the latter clad with a silver-grey mosaic fascia, and plenty of planting, though for the most part designers had run the gamut of plant display by now, leaving it as the province of last-minute stand fitters. Lewis's stand earned the ultimate accolade from George Grenfell Baines in *The Builder*: 'it makes you long to use their material.'

For the fourth exhibition in succession Cassidy, Farrington and Dennys did a sensitive stand for Cape Building Products, this time collaborating from the outset with the artist Merlyn Evans, who designed a three-dimensional mural in coloured Asbestolux. The Timber Development Association, for the first time since Roger Walters's stand of 1949, gave up its series of dramatic timber structures in favour of a simple rectangle. And the RIBA, through whose headquarters a new broom had recently swept, took steps at last to enliven the 'sepia-tinted morgue' they used as clubroom.

A problem not all designers solved was fitting their stand under the overhanging gallery. Alan Diprose boldly took this on for Bellrock Gypsum Industries, filling the whole space with a smart black and white horizontally timbered stand, strong and simple. If nothing much of the product was visible, at least its fine staircase with its glimpse of the first floor invited the visitor to satisfy his curiosity instead of seeming, as enclosed stands sometimes did, to say 'Keep Out'.

Stillman and Eastwick-Field again showed their mastery of stand design with two stands. For Concrete Ltd., there was a grey and black concrete stand (**102**) with red relief, the frame consisting of balanced cantilevers on a central system of columns, and hanging from it a virtuoso concrete stair ending one tread clear of the ground. Their stand bore a distinct family resemblance to their main architectural work of the period, as witness the Student

Union at Keele University, 1963. *The Builder* newspaper meanwhile celebrated its new format by commissioning from Stillman and Eastwick-Field a deliberately inexpensive and ephemeral stand (**100**). Their solution was to produce a strong stand in prefabricated timber, its impermanence underlined by the way the members were carried out several inches beyond the joists. The upper rooms were enclosed in panels of fibre-glass fabric brightly lit from inside, the floor was of pine board and the ceiling of white-painted slats.

Three other stands came in for special praise; Gordon & Ursula Bowyer's for Crane Ltd., Ryder and Yates's for the Gotham Group, and Dewar-Mills Associates' for Adamsez. Dewar-Mills, who did stands also for Ruberoid, Durasteel and the Architectural Press, produced for Adamsez a two-floor black and white stand (**101**) with a pyramid roof and a floor of different-sized glass marbles, sparklingly lit from below, out of which rose like plants free-standing sanitary fittings on white stalks.

1961

Dr Charles Hill, the newly appointed Minister of Housing, laid stress in his 1961 opening speech on the commonsense of teamwork right through, adding that members of the team not always remembered were the client, the user and the passer-by. It was a time of some buoyancy in the industry, and the exhibition broke all records both for size and for attendance.

Of the two special themes of high importance, one has long been comprehensively victorious while the other still battles on. The first involved the improvement of trade literature, concentrating on standardised format to international paper sizes – a glance at the literature on the stands showed how unhandleable for filing purposes it was, though the exhibition catalogue set a proper example – and on pre-classification by the Swedish SfB system. There was a model SfB library, organised by John Brunton, and an infelicitously named SfBee Hive. The second theme, again with special displays, was Design for the Disabled where Mrs Molly Montgomery was the driving force. The outcome was a grant to the architect Selwyn Goldsmith from the Polio Research Fund, strongly supported by the Building Exhibition itself and by the RIBA, which bore fruit in his influential book *Designing for the Disabled*. At the same time the Ministry of Housing took as its subject an allied theme in an extensive exhibit on Designing and Building for Older People.

For many years there had been comments about the desirability of sectionalised grouping of exhibits so that the visitor with a special interest could go straight to one area of the exhibition and carry out on-the-spot comparative studies. The arguments in favour were plain enough, but before satisfying them the organisers had to take into account the physical characteristics of the hall, the need for solid floors and wide entrances for the machinery and plant sections, and for extractors over the heating and fuel appliance sections, and much more besides, not least the fact that the whole exhibition had to be built in ten days. But 1961 showed some further movement towards the grouping of readily classifiable products, and the merits of synthesis were demonstrated in the Finnish and Swedish government displays, where a total of forty-five firms had their exhibits grouped into a planned whole.

Stands generally were lighter and simpler, framing rather than dominating the display. There were, reported one commentator,

fewer flowers and less string, although these commodities linger on among the second-rate stand-fitters'

designs. The idea of letting the materials form the display has at last caught on generally.

One famous company, however, put out an apparently straight-faced statement that 'in view of the heavy demand their own products had not been used in the construction of their stand.'

Many experienced designers again showed this year, but the increasing dominance of specialist exhibition firms was noticeable. Thus though architects Edward Mills and Dewar-Mills Associates had six and three stands respectively, the display firms Olympia Exhibitions and Beck and Pollitzer did half a dozen or more each.

Among the designers who had long worked for the same exhibitor was Kenneth Lindy, who had established a highly regarded house style for the National Federation of Building Trades Employers. His 1961 stand, on a long site, comprised an extre-

mely simple and open canopied space, enlivened by concealed diagonal lighting and display screens on the same diagonal to welcome the enquirer in. A new feature was the installation of information telephones on the stand.

Two-storey stands were by now commonplace, and the year saw the arrival of the first three-storey stand, from Brockhouse Steel, designed by D. E. Blayney. The most remarkable stand (**104**) however was designed by Ove Arup & Partners for Butterley, manufacturers of Aglite aggregate for use in prestressed and precast concrete structures. Using this lightweight high strength aggregate, finely finished, Arup produced an open springing curve, splayed outwards and enclosing a single stairway to a viewing platform. The whole was made of precast units all of different lengths but from the same mould.

Eastwood went to Robert Gutmann of the Design

105. London Brick Company, 1961: John R. Harris.
London Brick Co.
106. Pilkington, 1961: S. M. Sternfeldt. *AP.*

1961–1963

Research Unit for a timber and coloured panel stand, the frame divided at ground level by free-standing brick displays and the whole announcing its presence with a slender brick pylon twice the height of the two-storey stand. Clearly brick manufacturers were not feeling it necessary to follow the advice of *The Architect & Building News* to let the product form the stand. John R. Harris for London Brick (**105**), for instance, had a black steel and wood frame with a dark floor acting as foil for a series of glass panels on which were colour transparencies of jobs done with LBC bricks, and the bricks themselves displayed in sunk panels.

Two stands which caught the eye were those for Bellrock by Alan Diprose and Adamsez by Dewar-Mills Associates, both of whom had designed their companies' stands previously. Against a strong horizontal black and white background Diprose set a group of plastic forms, predominant among them a sweeping spiral cut at the top and ringed by a staircase. Stylish in themselves, these sculpted forms were ideal settings for the company's plasters. The Dewar-Mills stand (**103**) was contained within a palisade of tall white panels, spaced to allow glimpses of the interior, where a black cylinder enclosing a spiral stair rose from a red floor to a floating dark blue roof, ideal foils for the white china ware on display. Pilkington's house architect S. M. Sternfeldt produced a lavish box steel-and-timber frame (**106**) to show the glittering brilliance of the product. The cladding glass was coupled with mirrors to give the effect of doubling the area, and the upper floor was enclosed by faceted screens built up simply by bolting members (and readily dismantled). Even in the model shown here the entrance front is clearly a virtuoso turn; finished and fully lit, it was a dazzling fairyland.

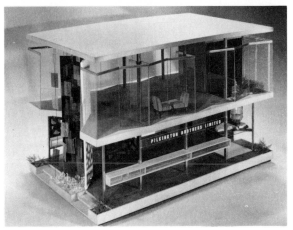

1963

Opening the 1963 exhibition, Geoffrey Rippon, Minister of Public Building and Works, transmitted the encouraging message that construction expenditure in the public sector would rise to a record level. The Exhibition itself had been formally re-named the International Building Exhibition, with the catalogue appearing in five languages. Since early days there had been a scattering of overseas exhibitors and in 1963 the numbers were still modest, but they were on course for the total of over 150 which they reached twenty years later.

Selwyn Goldsmith's book *Designing for the Disabled*, which had its genesis in the 1961 exhibition, had just been published, and the organisers invited him to mount an Accidents in the Home display. The year's major theme however was *Industrialisation Interpreted*, an ambitious series of stands under the supervision of David Rock of Building Design Partnership. Among the contributors were the trade associations, the MOPBW, and twenty-two companies working for the most part in concrete. Its success in getting across the message of standardisation and prefabrication was variously assessed: 'a brilliant success in bringing order to hundreds of different facts and facets,' said one journal; 'fairly incomprehensible,' said another.

The Architects' Journal (27 Nov. p. 1112) commented on the increasing part being taken by government at the exhibition, and on its much higher quality.

In the immediate post-war years the 'presence' of the architect at the Exhibition was mostly to be seen in the design of a handful of stands. Now, nearly twenty years later, the design of stands has on the whole declined and the architect's presence is being exerted mainly through the Ministries. It is a good exchange.

108. Merchant Adventurers, 1963: Paul Boissevain. *AP*.
109. Brockhouse Steel, 1963. *AP*.

1963

However that may be, the Government stands, co-
ordinated as a whole by A. Whitehead of the COI,
played a major part in the industrialisation theme.
The Ministry of Housing showed a high-density
low-rise scheme by J. H. Napper and Partners and
a Taylor Woodrow Anglian·development for the
LCC, the Ministry of Education showed system-
built schools in Hertfordshire together with explica-
tions of CLASP and SCOLA, MOPBW showed the
Nenk system, the Ministry of Health had a modular
display, the Building Research Station explained
the critical path method, and the GPO displayed the
fine new look they were giving to their standardised
Post Office vending and posting units.

W. H. Saunders this year took over the design of
the Eastwood Group's stand, and produced an open
frame surmounted by a series of high plain white
arches which directly echoed Basil Spence's work at
Sussex University. A newcomer, about to achieve
fame with vastly more substantial work, was
Richard Seifert. He neatly contrived a stand tucked
under the gallery for H. & R. Johnson, with tiled
ceiling, tiled lettering, tiled mural and, in an effective water feature, underwater tiles. 'Full of subtle
art and wit,' George Grenfell Baines found it,
naming it his favourite stand for the year.

Crittall, who had been exhibiting regularly for
more than half a century, this year had a stand (**107**)
designed by Bernard Lamb which comprised two
tall and light-filled silver and glass towers of different heights over a black floor and against a black
wall. The towers had jointed angles like a child's
climbing frame and there was no shortage of visitors
climbing up and down their various stairs.

Brockhouse Steel, back to a single storey again
this year (**109**), were among the few exhibitors to
pick up the theme of industrialised building. They
showed large CLASP photos and smaller back-lit
coloured transparencies, on an open framed stand
with a black box rib and white ceiling, a dark floor

and brilliant orange easy chairs. Running out from under the gallery, the whole made a straightforward and roomy-seeming statement.

Just as simple was Merchant Adventurers' stand (**108**) by Paul Boissevain. Within a well-proportioned open steel frame were four screen panels, much smaller in height and width than the stand itself, so that they punctuated it rather than partitioned it off. On the screens and the ceiling were sparingly grouped the company's light fixtures in a cool display a million miles from the garish nightmares which remain the hallmark of most commercial lighting retail outlets.

Staff architects designed the stand for Yorkshire Imperial Plastics. Contrasting with the heavy steel girders overhead, the display was made up almost exclusively of pipes, with the company's initials as an identifying mural, a screen wall composed of a great variety of sawn-off pipes and a lighthearted pipe sculpture. Certainly, whatever the problems elsewhere, there was no difficulty here in spotting what the company's products were.

1965

By 1965 the great Sixties building boom was well under way. The exhibition was opened by Harold Wilson, the first Prime Minister to perform this role. After paying special tribute to Mrs Montgomery for 'her enterprise and skill in developing export markets', he announced a target of half a million houses a year by 1970, and the creation of a pool of houses and flats for rent. This programme, he said, would need prefabrication in the factory, fast continuous production schedules and the minimum of design variation within a single scheme.

Following the success of his *Clean and Decent* exhibition in 1957, Lawrence Wright organised

Hot or Not, a display on heating through the ages based on his book *Home Fires Burning*. Another special display was *Artists and Architecture*, designed by Hilary Chambers to show the work of artists interested in working within an architectural context and the importance they attached to doing this right from the outset of the job. Carters of Poole, which had been exhibiting, with a succession of distinguished stands, for more than sixty years, linked up this year with the tile firm of Pilkington (not to be confused with the St Helens glass company). Together they produced a joint stand, an unroofed display designed by Christopher Read, house architect to the Carter Group, which radiated outwards from an off-centre tiled tower. Another shared stand was that of the Lead and the Zinc Development Associations, a well-detailed and stylishly lettered display by Dewar-Mills Associates, who had done a joint LDA/ZDA stand since 1961. Other regular clients of Dewar-Mills included the Architectural Press, Adamsez and Ruberoid; indeed, their association with the Architectural Press, continuous from 1953 to 1975, may well be the longest client/architect association in the Exhibition's history.

It was natural enough that most exhibitors wanted a new stand every time, even if the result was sometimes little more than a minor variation on an originally successful theme. *The Builder* however experimented with the opposite view, deliberately running the same stand for three consecutive shows. In 1961 John Rae designed for them a modular grid, consciously simple to contrast with the prevailing mode of highly-coloured and intricate displays all round them. In 1963 some rearrangement of the aisles at Olympia forced the designer into a number of modifications and redistributions of internal spaces, including closing the stand on two sides instead of the original one. And in 1965, the agreed last year of the stand's life,

the whole thing was face-lifted without regard to the austerity of the original design, and staff and students from the Hornsey College of Art applied a generous range of brilliant colours.

Dewar-Mills's stands provide a series of illustrations of the value of a well worked out colour scheme. Another example was Keith Townend's stand for Powell Duffryn Heating. A steel frame on two floors, it was quite lacking in any fastidious detailing, relying on the broad effects of bold colouring in black, white and orange. The lettering on the end wall was created by being sunk behind the wall surface, filled with orange mesh and lit from within.

John R. Harris broke new ground in his design (**110**) for London Brick. The back wall and two inset displays showed brick panels; the stand's overall effect was consciously that of a film set. Scaffolding supported a great battery of 'showboat' light

bulbs which spelled out the company's initials, whilst on the square plywood floor were red tables and a set of traditional Hollywood folding chairs with names emblazoned on the back. It could all scarcely fail to arouse the passer-by's curiosity.

Notable was another of Ryder and Yates's finely plastic stands (**111**), this time for British Gypsum. It comprised two contrasting elements: a two-storey box, open below, the enclosed upper section on its pilotis lit by a huge cluster of suspended and coloured fluorescent rods; and an open-ended oval-sectioned reception and enquiry area. Down one side of this ran a head-high viewing slit, and down the other a continuous information panel display leading the visitor through to the generous open space beside the box. The overall plan embraced Olympia's iron Corinthian column so that, far from seeming obtrusive, it stood comfortably with cube and oval.

112. Universal Asbestos, 1967: Edward D. Mills. *E. D. Mills.*
113. Componex, 1967: Building Design Partnership (David Rock and Stuart Beatty). *AP.*

Again there was an extensive grouped government display. Outstanding here was the GPO stand by the graphic designers Minale Tattersfield. Three massive cylinders were suspended over a grey carpet. There was nothing taxing about the GPO's message, and their stand got it across at once, giving visual pleasure as it did so.

1967

Although Anthony Greenwood, Minister of Housing, was able to report a record year for housing at the opening of the 1967 exhibition, things were far from well and, just as in the middle of the 1957 exhibition major capital investment cuts were announced, so, ten years later, the exhibition had been open only a week before the devaluation of sterling took place.

The dominant feature marking out the exhibition as a memorable one greeted the visitor at the entrance to the Grand Hall. This was Componex, a multi-storey building frame which aimed to provide a general picture of what the industrialisation of building meant in practice by exhibiting components in real situations. For the first time the products of 260 companies, chosen for their compatibility with the overall design, could be seen not in isolation but grouped in their building assembly context. Co-ordination stretched to the point of ensuring that all products on display were described, on A4 sheets, in a standardised and systematic way. The whole huge enterprise (**113**), which covered 4,000 square feet through five levels, was under the control of David Rock, with his Building Design Partnership colleague Stuart Beatty as project leader; and during the final three-month run-up a team of twenty-four from

BDP were working fulltime on the job.

In the event this imaginative and boldly planned project was bedevilled by difficulties. Components were not always supplied to time or even, sometimes, to the right scale, and this was bound to impose strains on the military-operation time-tabling always essential in organising exhibitions at Olympia where no overspill of time at either end could be allowed. The crippling blow however came from labour troubles with the hall's assembly crew. An unofficial but all-powerful veto on shift working was imposed. The erection contracts of City Display Ltd, in charge of site assembly for the whole operation, were dependent on round-the-clock shift working, with the consequence that the ambitious display was not complete by opening day.

Of course there were those ready with sardonic comments about this unlooked for injection of familiar on-site realism. But most people agreed that it was wretchedly bad luck and shared the view of *The Architects' Journal* that the directors 'should be congratulated on this imaginative venture. We hope they will develop it further and not be put off by the hideous embarrassments this first try-out seems to have caused.'

Beyond Componex there were interesting stands by Theo Crosby for Cape Building Products, Alan Tye for Allied Ironfounders (**114**) (an object-lesson in how to fit and light a stand under the gallery of Olympia), Hilary Chambers and Geoffrey Holland for the Cement & Concrete Association and Peter Bender for ICI, and much else besides, not all of it reflecting the spirit of the late 1960s. A wrought-iron stand, for instance, had as its centrepiece an iron bas-relief of the Last Supper. Once again Dewar-Mills produced an outstanding design for Adamsez, but some competition in this product area came from Ideal Standard. Conran Design

did a curious stand for them, the rectangular goods placed very four-square with an arched and strongly curved surround of orange and blue. Were these arches designed to suggest Gothic? Or Islamic? They were puzzling; and perhaps that was the intention.

Edward Mills, one of the most prolific and consistent of stand designers, did his fifth successive stand (112) for Universal Asbestos. Two storeys high, he gave it a red ceiling to create its own private sky beneath the unsympathetic roof of Olympia. Reaching up to this ceiling were fluted and corrugated asbestos panels, the fascia was moss-green with its graphics profiled in end-section, and the furniture was all natural pine.

Most of the important stands this year were, like Universal Asbestos, two storeyed. An exception was the design by Jack Howe and Partners for Redland. This was a large stand (115) with open space above,

penetrated only by sculptural vertical slabs at each corner. These slabs, impassive in themselves but projecting the company's name in their graphics, gave the stand, especially with its counterpoised and smaller tilted slabs, an eyecatching grandeur. The whole was tied together by an unadorned black fascia and ceiling over a rich grey carpet.

Characteristic of stand design at this time was the work of Towning Hill & Partners for Alumin (116). This was a white stand on a dark blue carpet, very clearly demonstrating the product, with the enclosed white first-floor box relieved by its graphics and by two tall slim vertical windows, which at one and the same time gave visitors a view over the exhibition and passers-by a hint that there might be something worth seeing up there. Obdurately resisting design skills, however, were those mosaiced photographs of mostly unappealing buildings showing the product in use.

As to official and professional stands, *The Architects' Journal* found a real falling off in interest. Government displays were no longer concerned with transmitting technical information but simply with putting over very simple messages. The Exhibition Department of the COI put together what the paper admitted was a pleasant environment, centred on a 'tunnel of love'; but it did not seem aimed at the industry and offered 'little or nothing for anyone with a serious interest in building.' The trade association and professional society stands fell short in a different way. The Electricity and Gas Councils at least showed recent developments; but most stands in this area were content simply to describe what their sponsors did and show their publications. The results were predictably dull.

1969

Two years later in 1969 the Minister of Public Building and Works, John Silkin, adroitly sidestepped in his opening speech the gloomy prospects facing the industry. Instead he concentrated on exports – contracts steadily growing, a record level of materials exported, British design consultants working in more than ninety countries – and he threw in a call, too, for more industry-financed research and development. As these calls to arms resounded through Olympia there was no lack of comment on the absence, for the first time, of government stands, particularly since the exhibition's special theme was the crucially important one of metrication. The stands themselves continued to do their job, or to demonstrate the variety of ways in which exhibitors thought they could promote their product. And in their comparative tameness they showed too the reaction there had been in the previous twenty years against emphasis on the stand itself as an object worth scrutiny in its

117. TRADA, 1969: Michael Tucker Associates. *AP.*
118. Industrial Communication Consultants, 1969:
Dargan Bullivant. *AP.*

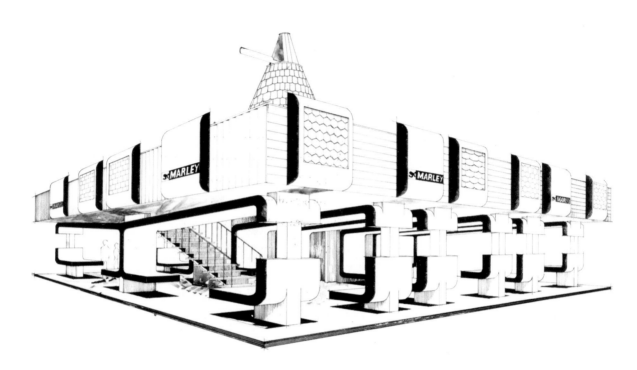

own right. Most of the familiar varieties could still be found: the worthy (in great numbers), the merely run-up, the ingenious, the traditional, the overbearing, the elegant, the discreetly luxurious and the indiscreetly opulent, the pleased-with-itself-and-good-luck-to-the-product, the talking showcase.

An admirably economical stand (117) was the one designed by Michael Tucker Associates for the Timber Research & Development Association (TRADA). Unencumbered by a ceiling, small-scale timber posts carried frames proclaiming their metric message round the perimeter of the stand. Inside, models were on display, and that was all, the whole thing readily demountable and reusable. The illustration shows how neighbouring stands could intrude at Olympia. The huge legend CONCRETE frowns over the back of the stand, whilst an array of more than life-size figures is

suspended over the side gangway. These figures are plastic banners for the *Profile of an Industry* exhibition across the gangway. Initiated by the exhibition organisers, co-ordinated by David Rock and designed by RCA student Jon Weallans, this display was a collaborative statement of the various career possibilities which the industry offered, each aspect with a specially designed (and sharply criticised) information desk under its banner and staffed by the appropriate professional or trade educational body.

Another display (118) concerned with information rather than the promotion of products was that of Industrial Communication Consultants. This was a technical literature design and production consultancy run by the architect Dargan Bullivant, who himself designed their striking stand. No luxury chairs here, hinting at a lavish hospitality area tucked discreetly away; just simple off-the-peg

stools. The whole stand showed that effectiveness
is not dependent on high budgets. It was not much
bigger than a coin-operated passport photograph
booth, but its brilliant lighting and scarlet curtains
made sure that its message was not overlooked
among its more opulent neighbours.

A problem likely to come the way of the designer
at any trade fair is that of incorporating unyielding
traditional features, trademarks, outmoded logos
and the like, within an imaginative design. Marley's
traditional oasthouse was a case in point. This year
the Marley Tiles Exhibition Department went all
out for a modern stand (**119**), one where, in the
event, the repeating shapes seemed to dwarf the
products themselves, and where the form chosen
gave a worrying hint of pincers snapping. Rising at
the rear was the statutory oasthouse. It may have
looked in uneasy alliance, but it towered over the·
stand, and proclaimed the familiar presence of

Marley clear across the hall.

There was no dispute about the year's outstanding display. This was the Cape Universal Building
Products stand (**120**), by Crosby Fletcher Forbes,
soon to take the name of Pentagram Design (see
page 103). Against a brilliantly lit wall screen the
products were arranged as a series of sculptured
and patterned totems with just enough lighting to
bring out texture and form. The products were
right in front of you; you could touch them; but,
equally, their arrangement was an affectionately
witty comment on the sculpture exhibitions at the
Institute of Contemporary Arts. Bird song could be
heard issuing from one group of products – until
neighbouring stands complained – and the whole
assemblage was triumphantly planned to do a
number of things at once: to gratify, or perhaps to
provoke the solemn (for there were commentators
who gave no hint of the fun Crosby was having),

121. British Steel Corporation, 1971: Kevin Goold. *AP*.
122. Delta Capillary Products, 1971: Jeff Tutin of
Clement Franks and Powell. *AP*.

to entertain the light-hearted, and – the real point – to arouse curiosity and so catch the attention of information seekers, for whom admirable facilities had been installed.

1971

Some measure of prosperity had returned by 1971, although the Vietnam war, the troubles in Northern Ireland, and a series of strikes at home raised questions about its continuance. But the industry, reported Peter Walker, Secretary of State for the Environment, in his opening speech, was on the move again following the introduction of improvement grants, tax reductions, a drop in mortgage rates and the end of the credit squeeze.

The theme of the exhibition was Research and Development. This emerged, however, far more in the conferences which had long been a valuable part of the exhibition than in the displays of exhibitors, who this year numbered 630 from eleven countries.

A change was coming over the pattern of stands. Or, more precisely, an element of patterning was creeping into the free-for-all in the increasing use of shell stands. These skeletal groupings produced a measure of order by providing the same external pattern for a whole segment of stands whilst allowing the manufacturer freedom to develop individual displays within his particular part of the overall shell. But the restricted space which made them economically attractive hindered attempts to mount displays of any complexity. Stuart Beatty and Hilary Chambers were among the most successful architectural practices which designed shell stands for the Exhibition from the late 1960s on.

The use of two-storey stands as a means of

winning attention and prestige had largely fallen away, but, perhaps as part of the economic upturn, they began to return in 1971. The most striking example was the British Steel Corporation stand (**121**) by Kevin Goold, conceived less as an ephemeral exhibition stand than as a well-designed and solid building. The red-lead stanchions allowed for display panels on the ground floor while supporting an upper floor faced throughout in vertically striped cladding. There was no hint to the visitor of what took place behind this.

1971 was the first year in which all the construction departments of government had been brought together as the Department of the Environment. The DOE stand, designed by Kenneth McDowall of the COI, stood at the entrance to the exhibition and capitalised on this by creating its own gateway effect, leading into tunnelled avenues containing multi-screen film projections. Similar use of the

tunnel motif was made by Jeff Tutin of Clement Franks and Powell for Delta Capillary Products (**122**). He created a simple walk-through tube, right-angled and irresistible, though its effectiveness would have been strengthened by a firmer statement of the product on display.

Alcan Booth Industries brought in the sculptor Ferris Newton for the overall concept of their stand, to be constructed of the manufacturer's own products. He produced an open ground floor, aluminium-framed, with a terrace above, reached by a highly assertive giant-scaled trellis staircase. But again too little attention seems to have been paid to getting the manufacturer's name across.

Forticrete used real concrete blockwork for the walls of their stand (**123**), by Tony Maher. The display screens in the maze structure between these light grey walls were black and white, and roof and ceiling had multi-coloured striping. The roof also carried a prominent indication of the product's name so as to catch the bird's eye view from the Gallery. The effect of this, and the virtual lack of other exhibitors who remembered to do the same, is well seen in the general view (**124**) of the exhibition from the gallery, with the British Steel Corporation stand on the right and, just visible at the far end, the Marley stand, for the first time lacking its traditional oasthouse motif.

Interbuild

1973

In 1973 the exhibition, now called Interbuild, was opened by Geoffrey Rippon as Environment Secretary, as ten years previously he had opened it as Minister of Public Building and Works. Fifteen per cent of the exhibitors were newcomers, and twenty-one countries were represented, the highest number to date. The theme was Environmental Services, and there were two special D O E displays, on Highways and on Kitchen Planning.

By now a shift in the approach to stand design was increasingly apparent. Manufacturers were by and large much less likely now to go to architects for their stands, preferring to use one of the mushrooming design studio firms or to put the clock right back to the unsophisticated days by doing any designing in-house even if, as the results sometimes suggested, they could not lay claim to much in the way of design talent. Naturally architects were the first, though they were not the only, people to lament the all too predictable results of this shift.

The generally depressing standard of the show [commented *The Architects' Journal*, 5 Dec. p. 1364] is reflected in the large number of exhibitors who are surprised to be asked who designed their stands. 'We did it ourselves' is the most common answer and when pressed further it turns out that 'we' means the people manning the stand.

Not to commission professional design skills for an exhibition like Interbuild was particularly short-sighted since the very people likely to specify the products on offer had aesthetic expectations which it would be merely prudent to try to satisfy.

The Brick Development Association recognised this in Andrew Bain's spacious stand (**125**), which included not only a display of brick set in a sequence of tall sculptural panels but also an imaginative show of provoking and none too serious sculpture recounting a day in the life of Lady Sarah Wellington-Gore. Lady Sarah was an elegant and liberated beauty invented by the sculptor Walter Ritchie, who was developing the technique of designing curved sculptural brickwork, and this exhibit was carried out with a most winning grace; he set it amongst a massing of flowers and fountains luxuriant enough to suggest that mockery was not far away. Ritchie's Lady Sarah series is now on public display in the gardens of Delapré Abbey, Northampton.

For all its mastery there was a welcome element of wit here, as there was too in Theo Crosby's unsolemn stand for Cape Universal Products. A large stockade, enticingly lettered and decorated in the Pentagram manner, led the visitor to an interior where he found the products, some notably pretty girls, a daily competition, and Crosby-designed plastic bags for his trade literature. This all ensured that he would not forget Cape.

Wit of a different kind appeared in Peter Murray's little stand for the paper *Building Design*, of which he was the editor. Positioned close to the main entrance, it staked all on a single idea by being sheathed in brilliantly coloured reflecting Melinex

125. Brick Development Association, 1973: Walter
Ritchie, sculptor. *BDA.*
126. New Zealand Government, 1973: Bruce
Whattam. *AP.*

127. Permutit, 1973: Priestley Studios. *AP*.
128. Precision Metal Forming, 1973: Brian Spearpoint. *AP*.

which proclaimed '*Building Design* reflects the scene.' And in Bruce Whattam's New Zealand Government stand (**126**) everything was again subordinated to a single idea. The goods were displayed half in, half out of packing cases with boldly stencilled labels to indicate that they had travelled across the world and would arrive ready crated at the specifier's doorstep.

The fact that an absence of any great amount of conscious design need not mean an ineffective stand was borne out by Priestley Studios' stand for Permutit (**127**). Well lit, sharply lettered, accessible, clean in outline, devoid of any groping for aesthetic effect and surely highly economical, it showed the picture frame disappearing so that the product could make its own immediate impact. Simple again was Brian Spearpoint's stand (**128**) for Precision Metal Forming. The steel cladding and decking sheets being promoted had no need of the all too familiar false ceiling of muslin overhead. A small selection of the company's sheets in brown and grey on a russet carpet reached up effectively into the huge roof area of Olympia, so often masked out or just ignored by stand designers.

1975

1975 was the thirtieth and last time the Exhibition was held at Olympia, its home since 1907. A new National Exhibition Centre, designed by Edward Mills, himself responsible for many distinguished stands at post-war Olympia exhibitions, was under way in Birmingham. Olympia was no longer large enough to house the Exhibition with any comfort, and the organisers were already separating off sections for independent display. In 1973 the first biennial International Woodworking Industries exhibition took place, and the first International Kitchen and Bathroom show was planned

for 1976. IWI continues as a major exhibition in its own right. So does what is now called Kitchens International, which is mounted alongside Interbuild in two of the eight halls of the NEC in Birmingham.

The growing concern of the mid-Seventies with alternative sources of energy was reflected in the exhibition's special feature on Ambient Energy, whilst homage was paid to European Architectural Heritage Year by a celebration of craft skills in place of machine technology. But the economic pendulum had swung right back and Reg Freeson, Minister of Housing, opened the exhibition against what the foreword to the catalogue itself called a 'background of severe economic restraint and a depression in the industry unmatched for thirty years.'

The recession showed itself at Olympia in the absence of some of the big name companies. For the visitor this was not an unalloyed loss. There was a welcome reduction in the customary clamour and pressure. Few double-decker stands were to be seen; in their place were many open displays with welcome circulation space round them. But the fact that the old lavishness was no longer to the fore provided evidence, both directly and by default, that when budgets are tight it is more important than ever to make the best use of stretched resources by employing a good designer. A stripped-down stand does not allow the sheer luxuriance of opulence to camouflage indifferent design.

Apart from the most lavish extravaganzas most kinds of stand were on display. Simplest was the box, in which the product was disposed with design added *ad lib*. They ranged from those plainly innocent of the very idea of design to the muted sophistication of Hilary Chambers' shell range (**129**) for the international section. Then there were

Interbuild

130. Metal Sections, 1975: JTL Advertising with Beck and Pollitzer. *AP*.

plenty of mock-up rooms, notably of course in the furniture and kitchens area, whilst D O E again used the walk-in method of successive panels unfolding within a maze, an attractive technique provided the visitor does not decide suddenly to retrace his steps. As always a number of stands were determinedly untouched by any breath of the contemporary. So this year a domestic fittings firm presented a two-storey Spanish villa, arcaded and pantiled, among whose sub-Alhambran splendours was a sleek display of sinks and cookers. Another firm offering the same range of products had a single-storey half-timbered building, its bow windows lace-curtained, its roof topped with plastic thatch. Perhaps it was the very fact that to peer through its windows seemed an invasion of rustic privacy which paradoxically did the trick. At all events the cottage was invaded day after day by crowds of baffled and curious visitors.

Finally came those stands where the product itself helped to form the structure. The Brick Development Association continued its adventurous series of stands with its architect Andrew Bain. Forty-one kinds of brick were used in the display, which included a tower from which water fell softly into a lily pond below, and a lofty yellow brick serpentine wall, which had to be prefabricated and assembled on the site.

Andrew Gagg of Clement and Street constructed Ash and Lacy's stand entirely by a striking use of their trapezoidal profiled steel sheeting Flocad, with plenty of circulation space beneath.

A more humdrum use of the exhibitor's product was made by JTL Advertising with Beck and Pollitzer for Metal Sections. Beams are not easy to display, but the designers of this stand (**130**) did not hit on the right solution when they hoisted the Metsec beams, the main object of the exercise, high

above the viewer's head. Gordon Proctor and Partners produced an effective and entertaining solution to a similar problem in displaying Selkirk Metalbestos stainless steel chimneys. They simply used them, set against mirror walls, as uprights for the stand itself.

1977

In 1977 the Exhibition moved, as planned, to its new home at the National Exhibition Centre in Birmingham. It was the first time all five halls of the NEC complex had been used for a single exhibition; and it was the biggest Building Exhibition ever, filling its new and altogether more upmarket site at a time when the fortunes of the industry were at their lowest ebb. But Peter Shore, the Environment Secretary, was able to congratulate

the industry on its export record, where it had achieved a 33 per cent increase, and to report his own success in getting more government money for building, especially for local authorities in inner city areas.

The export drive to the Middle East was now at its peak, and was reflected by a special section at the exhibition. Another section, devoted to renovation and improvement, was called Home Truths, whilst the Ambient Energy theme of 1975 was developed and updated, with the accent no longer on proselytising but on practical applications like flat plate solar collectors.

The new halls presented a different challenge to designers from the problems they had faced at Olympia. Gone were the jumbles of Hammersmith, the narrow gangways, the heterogeneous halls, the galleries, the ornate ironwork; in their place five impersonal factory-like halls. These provided a

132. Brick Development Association, 1977: Andrew Bain. *BDA.*
133. Hepworth, 1977. *Bdg.*

wholly neutral backdrop against which stands had to generate their own life and élan. On this first occasion not all designers met the challenge successfully.

But by this stage in the Exhibition's history only slight attention was paid to the design of the stand in itself, with a consequent decline in the designer's role. The stands of the 1950s, fruit of keenly competitive work among the country's top designers, had substantially yielded to a blandly stereotyped casing in which the product was displayed. The loss of accent on design had removed an excitement from the Exhibition – and the exhibitor's turning away from professional architectural skills had, quite incidentally, lost him a free consultancy service on his product in relation to the building process. Compared with twenty, or forty, years previously, there is significantly little record of designers' names, though Theo Crosby did another relaxed and lively stand for Cape Industries and Towning Hill an ingenious triangular structure for James Gibbons, who had been exhibiting since before the turn of the century.

Hepworth had a simple message: they make every kind of tube. And they proclaimed it in the nature of their stand (**133**), a huge open tubular structure studded with smaller tubes. By the expedient of leaving a generous opening at one side they transformed a potentially claustrophobic into a pleasantly novel experience. The workman in the illustration engaged in finishing off is a reminder of the ever-present and not always overcome hazard of completing on time.

British Steel's stand (**134**) had a single bold idea, which was not to show a particular product but to symbolise the massive strength and reliability of the company. The huge sculptural tubes were painted red, and they left an admirable amount of clear floorspace. But a stand must reflect absolute confidence and if the chance occurs it does not harm

even to hint at a touch of magic. On this stand the support rods tying the ends of each projecting tube to the floor speak unmistakably of belt-and-braces rather than of magic. They take the stand out of the 'look no hands!' world, and back anti-climactically to cautious reality. Moreover, the contribution of the wellnigh mandatory plant pot to the whole stand is open to question.

In his stand (**131, 132**) for the Brick Development Association Andrew Bain returned to the highly successful collaboration with the sculptor Walter Ritchie which he had initiated in 1973. Aiming to show both the structural versatility of bricks and their sculptural and decorative potential, they jointly achieved a stand with at least four elements to its complex interest, five if we include the generous amount of free space they brought about. Plain brick panels 20ft high fringed the office and information area. This led out to a group of inter-

locking one-brick-thick hoops and arches on a circular brick base. Beyond this again was a barley-sugar brick structure spiralling up one of the hall's columns and edged with a small pool and planted area (the least successful part of the stand). Ritchie's special contribution lay along the boundary of this area in the form of five brick panels in different degrees of relief depicting a day in the life of Atalanta the huntress (**146**). Like his 1973 series on the memorable if mythical Lady Sarah these combined elegance and wit with a frank sensuousness usually, and unsurprisingly, absent from the Building Exhibition.

1979

By 1979, when Michael Heseltine as Environment Secretary opened the exhibition, any hope that the

mid-Seventies recession might be a thing of the past had quite disappeared. We were faced, said the foreword to the catalogue, with 'government expenditure cuts at national and local level, a tailing off of new house starts, a current series of gloomy economic forecasts and falling workloads among the professions.' The workload downturn across the industry was ten per cent. In consequence, although there were 800 stands, observers noticed fewer innovative products than usual and little progress in the rise of new materials.

There was a big overseas presence, from Finnish building materials producers through the full-spate flood of kitchens from Germany and France to a group exhibit by nine Taiwanese companies. A number of major companies stayed away this year, though most were to return in 1981, and the cutbacks which were the cause of their absence were also responsible for a certain meagreness and lack

of verve in most of the stands. These, wrote Theo Crosby (*Bdg*, 7 Dec. p. 29),

are generally dominated by a yearning for economy, tempered only by outbursts of vulgarity. Few, especially among the British exhibitors, seem to have been seriously designed. Most followed the shell scheme and let the contractor do his usual worst.

There was a time when exhibition design was something which was given to the brightest young architects. It helped them to cut their teeth on something real but ephemeral, and it cost the manufacturers very little. Then – actually it was years ago – the contractors began to peddle design and exhibitors took to drink.

At Birmingham, he said, there seemed to be few stands in which the bar did not take pride of place.

But the educative function of the Exhibition was more marked than ever; in five days there were no less than fifteen seminars on subjects ranging from fire prevention and the problems of the inner city

to Prestel and computer-aided design. The communications revolution was a main theme of the exhibition. Contel, the computer store-phone network-home tv system, was in use on a number of information-oriented stands, and was commissioned by Interbuild itself to provide a daily exhibition news service.

The decline in sparkle and inventiveness among the stand designs naturally brought press comment which, even allowing for some disposition in favour of architectural input, was unchallengeable in its criticism. *The Architects' Journal* (12 Dec. 1949, p. 1268) for instance, noted that

whatever the quality of product those with the biggest audiences were invariably in the better designed stands. Some quite good products were overlooked by many visitors because of their unattractive setting. And the stands didn't have to be that good – just a bit more interesting, with the product well displayed. It showed quite clearly that stand design and settings are important for sales. Style is not necessarily more costly.

Unfortunately the journal did not discuss in any detail what it thought were the better designed stands; it listed only five out of the 800, and credited the designers of only three of them.

Alan Tye Design again did the Allgood stand, which had an overall integrity of design appropriate to a stand displaying the classic Modric ironmongery product range, designed by Alan Tye himself. British Steel had a Moon Base stand (**135**) largely made from its own products. A space ship which hovered over the stand, about to launch itself the length of the hall, gripped the attention, not least by the way it made some use of the space over the stand.

Conran Associates did a neat 'Housepack' instant-packaged-home stand for Habitat, but the most

striking stand (**136**) was the Italian one of Arclinea, kitchen manufacturer. Presenting the appearance of a simple packing crate and executed – the crate and the relief lettering on it – in sawn wood, it was nonetheless work of great sophistication, designed to tempt you irresistibly inside.

1981

John Stanley, the Housing Minister, opened the 1981 exhibition in optimistic mood, hymning the virtues of flexibility and competition. The industry, he claimed, was in good heart and highly resilient, and he listed a number of major export successes.

Product manufacturers were still concentrating their fire on the oil-rich Middle East, but the industry as a whole had few signs of recovery to show, and spirits were not raised by the introduction during the week the exhibition was open of a sombre mini-budget.

The major trade associations, Cement & Concrete, Brick, Timber, were absent, though they all returned in 1983. Nonetheless 1,200 companies were battling for attention and an encouraging number of innovative products was reported. It was the biggest building exhibition ever held in the English-speaking world, and its tally of visitors was up by seventeen per cent on the previous record, some of them perhaps taking *The Architects' Journal* advice on how to meet the demands of the huge Centre by kitting themselves out with stout, sensible shoes, light clothing, a rubber-tipped shooting stick and a hip-flask.

With disturbingly few exceptions [the same journal pointed out, 2 Dec. p. 1092] stand designs are over-elaborate and crudely executed – often at the last moment by desperate junior executives. Some of the display techniques would have looked out-moded in the mid-50s . . . There was only a handful of decent

stands and they were all successful for the same reason: product, stand design, and graphics were all working in harmony to project a clear, hard-edged 'image'.

And the writer commented on the mismatch between product and stand, usually to the detriment of a good product, less often where a well designed stand did something to rescue a poor product. There must however have been an element of putting a brave architectural face on things behind the claim that slimmed down budgets had resulted in awareness of the need to 'put across a strong message without expensive or frivolous trappings.'

Of course traditional trappings of these two kinds were still in evidence in the expedients used to entice visitors of varying tastes, from scantily clad models to racing cars. But Interbuild set up a series of awards to show how exhibitors could make themselves more effective and competitive through the use of design, while at the same time encouraging

recognition of the part professional designers play in the building industry; and the publicity the winners received was a substantial extra prize. The judges, under the chairmanship of Lord Reilly, for many years a distinguished Director of the Design Council, were drawn from the RIBA, the Royal Society of Arts, the Design Council and the Society of Industrial Artists and Designers. Their criteria were overall appeal, value for money, creativity, innovation, fitness for purpose and ease of maintenance.

The best kitchen design award went to Arclinea (UK): designer Silvio Fortuna. Alan Tye Design was involved in awards for its stainless steel washbasins for the disabled, designed for W. G. Sissons, and for architectural ironmongery, developed jointly for G. & S. Allgood and Newman-Tonks. D. A. Thomas and Co. Ltd won the corporate graphic design for the literature on their Hewi

range and its incorporation into the stand design (literature designed by Brian Frost, their commercial manager). The best general building product award went to Ash and Lacy, who projected their message with a raked and curvilinear variation on their established success in designing their stand wholly from Flocad (**137**).

There were joint winners of the best stand design award, which went to Amstad Systems Ltd for the most effective use of their products as part of the stand structure, by Goodwyn Wheeler Associates, and to Zanussi's impeccable stand by the Swiss architect Michael Burckhardt. Burckhardt's stand (**139**) was essentially a dramatic frontage of semi-transparent fabric banners (every one bearing the company's name), suspended lighting and the outline of a structural frame.

Among other remarkable stands were those for Ideal Standard by Leslie Gooday, and for Patera Products by the architect Michael Hopkins and the structural engineer Tony Hunt. Patera's was a small stand built within the Interbuild shell system, containing nothing beyond some Eames chairs, a model, graphic panels and white reflective surfaces. Its significance was that it was an off-the-peg lightweight steel portal frame enclosure with the maximum usable internal space. This was an increasingly familiar form of enclosure in light industry, and in such structures as Norman Foster's Sainsbury Centre, a form which Hopkins and Hunt were closely associated with, and its appearance, immaculate and simple, at Interbuild could only help to broaden popular knowledge about it and to raise the level of industrialised systems generally. Certainly it aroused considerable interest.

1983

The Builder Group, whose stands over three-quarters of a century constitute an index of shifting

design tastes, had had a very unexciting stand in 1977. By 1981 Richard Negus designed a much more ambitious stand (**138**) which they shared with Barbour Index. And for their 1983 stand (**141**) they went to Rock Townsend, whose senior partner David Rock had had thirty years' experience of designing stands at the Exhibition, producing a series marked by an imaginative flair which unfailingly crossed that first crucial hurdle of coaxing the passer-by into stopping and looking.

Their 1983 stand formed a group of open partitions radiating from a central shaft and marked off one from another by head-high translucent panels taken from the components of a suspended ceiling system. Overhead the partitions were roofed with red and blue fabric ceilings, while surmounting all were white sails made of an elastic nylon which allowed them to form naturally into graceful double curves. The sails gave the stand an airy

elegance; their support and structure spoke discreetly of high technology; and their reaching up into the space above marked the stand out as among the very few breaking the monotonous single-storey skyline.

There was no sign of an end to the protracted recession, and as always the exhibition mirrored the economic climate. Many building products manufacturers made a welcome return in 1983, but the industry's *faute de mieux* emphasis on rehabilitation and make-do-and-mend was matched by the growing stress at Interbuild on interiors, on kitchens and bathrooms, and family parties were much more in evidence than in the past. But it was the biggest exhibition yet: 1,500 exhibitors from 28 countries; 79 trade associations represented; all seven halls filled for the first time; a growth of 25 per cent.

Pilkington were back, with a faceted glass struc-

ture (**143**) designed by Conran Associates and built in six days, and with the Pilkington green and white cross logo hoisted clear over the stand to beckon visitors. So, for the first time for more than a decade, were London Brick, showing as London Brick Products. Their thoughtful and spacious stand (**140**), by Trickett Associates, showed a wide range of colours and bonds of brick, decorated by blown-up working drawings. It was the joint winner with G. and S. Allgood of the Interbuild Award for the best overall stand design.

Post-Modernism put in an appearance in the fortified (and thus playing-on-its-name) stand for Castle Kitchens (**144**), a strange structure by Graham Jones of Contract Design which sat under the trussed girders of the hall's roof defiantly calling attention to itself. Poles apart in spirit was Broggi and Burckhardt's variation on their 1981 design

for Zanussi, again decorated with vertical yellow and black banners.

Tall vertical banners were also used in the prize-winning Allgood stand, this time, and very properly, recording not only the exhibitor's name but also that of the designer Alan Tye. Here (**145**) an open square was marked out, well in from the perimeter, by low black concrete walls with wide and hospitable openings in them. The five banners reached up to link the floor area with a giant white cloud-canopy suspended from the Hall roof and lit by uplighters in the concrete walls. The cloud was visible from every part of the hall, and the whole stand was emphatic proof that a well designed stand need not be complex. The only prerequisite, without which there is little prospect of success, is to call on the creative imagination of a good designer.

AFTERWORD
The Well-designed Stand

Many of the illustrations in this book show the stands in a fine isolation worlds removed from the clamour of the exhibition hall. They may be presented as drawings, like Arcon's stand for Finch, 1947 (**76**), or photographed by night like Dewar-Mills's Adamsez, 1959 (**101**), but the reality will be more like Arcon's Williams & Williams's stand, also of 1947 (**77**). In the real world the stand will find itself surrounded by competitors, all shouting or waving or seductively whispering as they try to divert attention from their rivals and onto themselves.

Every stand is an advertisement which tells the visitor how the company sees itself and invites him to share this view. No visitor is going to scrutinise a thousand stands, and it is the designer's key task to catch the sometimes flagging attention of the footsore as they trudge by, to persuade them then and there to make one more detour. They will do this only if their attention is captured at very first sight, and in a setting which subliminally helps to assure them of the quality of the goods and service offered. If the designer is not able to persuade them the point has gone and it doesn't much matter what else he does.

He is in effect an artist working (like so many other artists) in the world of advertising. There need be no clash between propaganda and aesthetics, but it is the first which, by a short but decisive head, is the final determinant of the stand's success. His design talents are directed by and subservient to the needs of the product and its display, and in this sense he is more like a stage designer than an architect. His job is to create as compelling an atmosphere and setting as the drama demands, however remote from his personal tastes the result may be. But unlike the stage designer, who is creating a middle-distance impression in the already heightened setting of a darkened theatre, his work will be walked through, probed and scrutinised at point blank range.

The visitor's direct contact with the stand and with the product gives the designer a challenge not usually found in the advertising world. But more than that: Interbuild speaks to a public itself professionally concerned with design. It is thus legitimate to use this concern as one way of attracting attention, by placing a degree of emphasis on the stand itself which in other contexts would be thought distracting or overbearing or irrelevant. Certainly architect-visitors are attracted by a good stand and repelled by a poor one. And because of this same professional concern the technical press is always likely to give space (and thus free publicity) to a well designed stand.

Of course exhibitions are temporary, but when they close that is not the end of things. Like the vapour trail marking the transit across the sky of a now vanished aircraft, a trail is left across the memory by a successful exhibition long after it has been dismantled. Forty years on those who saw it still hold a memory of *Britain Can Make It*, an exhibition of unobtainable goods which a million and a half people thought it worth queuing to see in 1945. And though memories of the actual event inevitably grow fainter and more diffuse, the exhibition's impact may colour a whole style of living, as did the 1951 Festival of Britain. The 1940s and 1950s were the highwater mark of British exhibition design. During much of this time the scarcity of other outlets for design innovation and imagination threw the magically unfettered world of the exhibition into particular prominence. Indeed, exhibition work did a good deal to sustain and nourish the art of architecture both through the long years of war and the post-war period of honourable high-minded propaganda for the new Jerusalem of social democracy.

The obvious and inescapable fact about stand design is its ephemeral nature, though even this is sometimes overcome by the design of remountable displays, like that for TRADA, 1969 (**117**) or Edward Mills's 1959 stand for Universal Asbestos, which the company later re-erected as a permanent Display Centre at its Tolpit works. The stand's short life brings certain advantages to its designer (beyond the fact that he does not have to live with his failures), and has done ever since the custom of apparently designing for ever lost favour, as in the Harland stand of 1913 (**16**) and the Gas Light and Coke stand of 1928 (**39**). It does not need to last long, it is in a setting sheltered from climatic stresses, and it is not shackled by building byelaws and the like, though it still has to satisfy the District Surveyor with regard to public safety. So economies and unorthodoxies can be freely introduced, along with materials, textures and effects not practicable outside.

The stand presents only minor problems compared with the usual work confronting the architect. But unlike that usual work it has not only to satisfy the senses but also, as we have seen, to win the battle of attention-seizing. How can this be done most effectively?

If the architect is lucky enough to be working with a suitable material, a highly effective course

is for him to use the product for constructing the stand itself. The brick companies have always done this, right from the days of Lutyens's Daneshill stand, 1909 (**13**). Skinner's Venesta stand of 1934 (**51**) was another notable example, and Ash and Lacy have been using Flocad for some years now both to construct their stand and to project their message (1975 and their prize-winning stand of 1981 (**137**)).

If his client has a strong brand image, the designer can reinforce it, comment on it, use it as theme for a set of variations; and he must hope that any logo or trademark will not clash too violently with contemporary design (Marley, 1969 (**119**)). Alternatively he can try for a single powerful icon or overriding theme (Delta 1971 (**122**), New Zealand Government 1973 (**126**)). Or he can make use of the special theatricality of the exhibition setting to create the startling, the deliberately improbable, of the kind usually excluded from the workaday world outside by the building regulations or the laws of physics or even the cautious rules of good taste (Carter 1955 (**90**), Lafarge 1949 (**79**)).

A less complex variation of this, given the talent, is to go for fun and fantasy, like Cape Asbestos 1969 (**120**) or for a simple witty approach like Yorkshire Imperial Plastics 1963. But surrounded by ever more hectic sophistication, the designer may decide to make his impact by going for the inexpensive, and the deliberately simple (Industrial Communication Consultants 1969 (**118**), Precision Metal 1973 (**128**)).

If at all possible he must try to fix in the visitor's memory an image which is identified with a specific product, with this company and not that one. Anyone who watches television can recall notable advertisements which nonetheless fall at the hurdle of imprinting the sponsor's name in the memory. Better to aim at the effect exemplified in the tale of the bar parlour sage who, in the midst of explaining that some people (like himself) were simply immune to the wiles of advertising, paused to order himself another Guinness because he knew it was good for him.

Associating the advertisement with the product name is always desirable, but in the exhibition world, where the stand is in effect the advertisement, the need is less insistent and the designer may decide instead to entice the passer-by with the intriguing or baffling or alluring and, having once caught him, leave the rest to the product display on the stand, the technical staff (who must *be* technically competent) and the trade literature (Arclinea 1979 (**136**)). Another approach, since people always want to see what is going on, is for the designer to catch their attention by having something happen on the stand, as with Sika, as long ago as 1930 (**44**).

Or he may decide to do none of these things, enrolling instead in the minimalist school which holds that the most effective approach to stand design is to create a setting so unobtrusive as to be wellnigh invisible as a separately identifiable element, so that nothing distracts the attention by coming between the onlooker and the product displayed (Permutit 1973 (**127**)).

The diversity of stands shown in this book and the diversity of the products they display point to the futility of any attempt to set out firm rules for stand design except of the most general kind – and even these general rules may be readily broken by a designer who is really in command of what he is doing. But whilst circumstances will allow the good designer to alter cases, there remain some general principles which should be taken into account.

Plainly the stand must appeal. If it fails here, the client has wasted his money. But appeal is no abstract concept. The stand need not appeal to schoolboys or avant-garde aesthetes or architectural critics. It is intended to attract a particular identifiable public and the character of that public must be carefully considered.

The purpose of the appeal is to capture attention, but to capture it not for the stand but for the product. The stand has to lead the visitor to the product, not get between them. And it must neither flatter the self-esteem of the designer nor pander to the whims of his client if, as occasionally happens, these are prejudiced or ignorant. Nor must it look as though it has been designed by (or for) a committee.

The stand should make the manufacturer's name inescapably clear, as some of those shown in this book do not. It should be congruent with the product and display a suitable fitness for its purpose. And it should be easy to maintain.

It must give value for money, and increased costs do not necessarily mean increased value. The case has been known of an in-house architect designing a spectacular succession of stands which finally became so expensive that his company withdrew altogether from the Exhibition for several years.

The stand must be easy of access, and offer the visitor a clear means of escape too. Usually it will extend an open welcome. But it is possible, though risky, for a skilled designer to contrive an enclosed box-like structure the very aloofness of which intrigues the visitor into investigating further.

It is sometimes said that the stand must avoid large areas which are not involved in promoting the product. But this is certainly better than clutter, and provided design skills have been properly used on the rest of the stand, the visitor may mark it as a bonus to the exhibitor that he has thought to offer as well an oasis of open space with somewhere to sit. The opportunity for a brief rest and discussion is always popular in the unforgiving acres of exhibition stands.

The architect must not think of the stand in isolation but must design it in its setting. It is going to take its place among a jostling crowd of competitors and, to put it at its most obvious, a design, however exquisitely detailed, which can be seen as a whole only from ten metres away will be – provided it needs to be seen as a whole at all – fundamentally flawed if the gangway is only three metres wide.

As well as displaying the product the stand is also demonstrating how the company sees itself. Often the only contact a visitor will have with the company, it must clearly project the strengths of head office and factory, and arouse expectations of overall quality, so every element, from the graphics to the sometimes neglected floor-finishes, calls for the most careful attention. Lighting too; but this presents its own particular snare to the designer. The form of the stand is often not best revealed, is sometimes actively concealed, by brilliant lighting, and textures designed for glancing light are often deadened by head-on glare. The lighting has to compete too with the known sources in the exhibition hall and with the unknown levels and angles from neighbouring stands.

But the great majority of stands have not been designed at all in a professional sense at any of the Building Exhibition's forty shows since 1895. The manufacturer has simply taken space and filled it up, either by getting his staff to do the job or by putting it out to a firm of stand contractors. The best of these, like City Display, have done very distinguished work; most have not. But the Exhibition is aimed at professionals and it is reasonable to use professional skills at it.

The client who intends to have his stand professionally designed may already have a house architect or an established relationship with an architectural practice with which he has worked successfully in other contexts. There may be a practice he knows and thinks likely to project the kind of image he wants, whether it is traditional, avant-garde or

points between. An architect's work for others at previous exhibitions may have caught his eye.

If he has not already settled on his designer he may turn to the RIBA's Clients' Advisory Service or to similar services run by the Design Council and the Society of Industrial Artists and Designers. An Appendix to this book prepared by the Exhibition organisers Andry Montgomery Ltd gives practical details on how to find, commission and work with a designer.

For his part the architect will welcome the job. It may be modest in scale, but it offers special pleasures. Traditionally it is an area where young architects can try out their wings. It gives them a unique opportunity to see a job through, with a minimum of restrictions, from start to finish in a matter of weeks. But many a solid, even stolid, architectural practice must have leapt at the prospect of experiment and excitement which stand design has given them.

Looking back over many years of exhibition design, Cecil Handisyde characterises the job as 'a pleasant nightmare.' A fuller analysis, which does not dissent from this view, appeared in a group of articles in *Building* from January to April 1949. The writer was Rodney Thomas of Arcon, the practice whose stands through the post-war years were unsurpassed in their invention, flair and sheer effectiveness.

An architect entering stand design for the first time finds himself plunged into the show business with all its rush and enthusiasm. [The rush results from the extremely short time allowed for erection, but he owns that even with more time the position would not be very different.] The designers would always get new ideas or think of some improvement, and still find themselves with too little time. It is this desire to do something better that makes exhibition atmosphere so pleasant. It is certainly worth doing at least one exhibition just to experience the intensity of the last few days

and nights. To begin with, everyone tolerates conditions of work that would never do normally. I think
this is due to the fact that everybody concerned has an
opportunity to exercise their own ingenuity, and the
work is novel and interesting. Exhibition work is probably the last stronghold of the individual craftsman.
The plasterers do moulded work instead of endless flat
surfaces, the joiners get curved work, and so on through
all trades. Every conceivable craft is represented,
painters doing murals or constructing designs out of
string, sculptors working in plaster or paper . . .

Exhibition work is temporary and, therefore, can act

as a physical sketchbook in which ideas can be developed
which may enrich the more disciplined side of architectural work.

And Thomas's summary of this 'pleasant nightmare'?

When everything is finished after several days and
nights of work, and, tired and dirty, you watch the
well-groomed salesman saunter in and take over, you
vow never to touch exhibition work again, and then
the next opportunity arises, and of course you do.

APPENDIX

How to work with a designer

How to choose a designer

General British industry and commerce are fortunate in being able to draw on the skills of one of the oldest, largest and best-trained bodies of designers in the world. As the first industrialised nation, Britain was the first to give rise to an organised profession of designers and its training system based on a network of schools of architecture, design colleges and polytechnics throughout the country, is second to none for its spread and breadth.

As with other professionals, designers tend to specialise in one or more of the fields covered by the profession. A high percentage practise on their own or in small groupings (which may be a convenient way of bringing together people with differing individual skills and talents), but the last thirty years have seen a great growth in the number of designers employed in a salaried capacity in industry or in commercial companies.

To find the right designer for the job, a client is well advised to study the designer's past work in the light of his own requirements. If a mutually satisfactory solution to the problem in hand is to be achieved, it is vital that designer and client should be able to work together with sympathy and understanding for each other's point of view.

Architects and industrial designers Architects and industrial designers share the same background of specialist training coupled with practical experience. They also follow a similar method of working, based either on a small (one or two man) office or on a larger grouping, which will probably include experts in a variety of design skills. While architects have traditionally tended to specialise in designing buildings they are increasingly involved in interior design work (including exhibition stands) and to some extent in products. Industrial designers range over a wide field from consumer and engineering products, through interiors and exhibitions to textiles and fashions and all aspects of visual communication.

This inevitably results in some overlapping both as between architects and industrial designers and within the more specialist disciplines. While the client's element of choice is increased, it also becomes more important for him to decide whether his particular problem can better be tackled by a large and more widely ranging practice or by a small and probably more specialised one.

Architects are almost certainly members of the Royal Institute of British Architects (RIBA). The equivalent chartered professional association for designers is the Society of Industrial Artists and Designers (SIAD). Both organisations are concerned with standards of performance, professional conduct and integrity. Membership is conditional upon adherence to codes of professional conduct, which among other things guarantee that information supplied by clients will be regarded as confidential. Corporate membership is a demonstration of the achievement of an appropriate degree of professional experience.

Engineering designers Some products, because of their complex mechanisms, require the services of engineering designers, who normally have a science-based training and may be members of one of the chartered engineering institutions or of the Institution of Engineering Designers (IED). Engineering designers are customarily less concerned with the overall appearance of the product than their industrial design colleagues, whose training is art-based. To achieve a satisfactory result, it is often necessary for the two specialists to work closely with each other, in which case the sooner they can be brought together the better.

In-house designer Many companies in recent years have decided to establish their own in-house design staff rather than buying in the services of design consultants as and when they are required. The advantage of an in-house designer is that he can be expected to be thoroughly familiar with your organisation and the fields in which it operates. The danger is that his area of vision will be restricted to these fields and that he may become 'stale' through lack of opportunity to broaden his range of skills by working with a wide variety of clients. He may be too used to knowing what you didn't like last time! He may not be able to argue and present the best case because of the existing hierarchy in the firm.

Your in-house designer will have come from the same background and gone through the same training as his freelance colleagues. He is just as likely to be a member of the relevant professional association (RIBA, SIAD or the chartered engineering institutions). To get the best advantage from his services, he should be made to feel that he has the ear of top management and should be brought in at the very start of the project, in the same way as a consultant. It is important that you should work *with* your in-house designer rather than give him the impression that he is simply being used. And remember that briefing him is as important as it is when dealing with an outside designer. Just because he is on the spot do not forget that he cannot read your mind and needs to know what you expect. So brief him if possible in writing and be precise about format, size, content, cost, delivery and so on.

Many of the same considerations also apply to in-house PR and press officers. There are solid publicity benefits to be gained from a well-designed stand or products and the advice of experts in this field should be taken at the early planning stage. They should also be kept informed as the work progresses so that as much advance publicity can be obtained as possible (e.g. in trade and technical press and in the design-oriented press as well).

Contractor/designer While the use of a qualified designer to carry out the entire design of exhibition stands is to be desired, it may well be that for a small interior in a shell scheme stand the cost of a design consultant is too high to be carried by your exhibition budget.

The alternatives are basically two. Firstly, to use a designer to provide the original concept and let the exhibition contractor complete the work under your supervision; secondly, to use the design facilities of an exhibition contractor whose design overheads are partially absorbed by his production profit.

In both of these cases, it is even more important to give a clear brief to the designer since in the first case you will have to implement the concept and you must make sure that this is within your capacity; in the second case the in-house designer is not acting solely in your interests, as your own consultant would be, and you must take care to watch that the 'cheap service' is not charged back at a premium.

Many printing companies have in-house facilities and will offer a graphic design service. Again this service is unlikely to be as good as an independent consultancy so you should be very clear in your briefing.

A designer's service

Working with a designer will follow this pattern:

Discussion of contract (including negotiation of fees);
Briefing;
Design work including:
Preparation and submission of preliminary design proposals;
Development of design proposals;
Preparation of finished working drawings and/or artwork;
Advice on and/or supervision of production.

There is no commitment between client and designer until the appointment has been confirmed (preferably in writing). Even then it is normal for the contract to provide that the commission may be terminated at any stage, subject to payment for the work carried out up to that point.

Scope of work

Discussion of contract At the initial meeting, the designer will need to be given a comprehensive account of the problem to be solved, together with an idea of any apparently conflicting requirements and of the timescale allowed. He must be given the opportunity to ask for the necessary information to enable him to estimate his fees and outside costs. It is in the interests of both parties that the understanding between them should be clear from the outset, to avoid difficulties that might otherwise crop up later on. Taking extra time at the beginning to make sure that the ground has been covered as fully as possible may well avoid wasting precious hours later sorting out problems that need not have arisen.

The designer may well have a set of standard conditions of engagement to which he works (such as those recommended by the RIBA or the SIAD) with any variations necessary to suit the particular contract. Alternatively, he may prefer to tailor the details each time in relation to individual commissions. Either way, when he has had a chance to consider the whole problem in the light of his existing work load, he will write you a contract letter.

This letter will set out the understanding reached about the terms of the commission and will state the stages through which the design process will pass, together with the fees due at each stage. The designer will also explain any additional expenses payable, such as travelling costs, long-distance telephone calls, bought-in materials etc (all of which are normally charged at cost) and will, where possible, estimate the length of time necessary to complete at least the first stage of the work.

One point which should not be overlooked at this stage is the position regarding copyright (and patents, where these apply). Remember, just because you pay for a design it does not necessarily become your property. The contract between you and the designer should state quite clearly whether, and if so at what point, the copyright is assigned to you by the designer (with whom it will originate) and whether a separate fee is payable. In the case of commissioned photographs, however, the position is different: here the copyright belongs to the commissioner, so that, if, for example, you pay a photographer to take a photograph of your stand, the copyright will belong to you.

The designer's contract letter should be studied very carefully to ensure that the understanding between you has been correctly set out and that his fee proposals are acceptable. The designer must not be expected to start work on the commission, however urgent it is, until these points have been agreed and confirmed in writing. The exchange of letters between you will then constitute the formal contract.

Briefing The importance of a clear and comprehensive brief for the designer cannot be over-exaggerated. It is not too much to say that the success of the job may well depend upon it, since it will guide the designer's thoughts and ensure that he is fully aware of the problem he is being asked to solve. It is therefore essential that all aspects of your firm's activities – marketing, production, costing etc – are involved from the beginning. This will prevent decisions being taken which later may have to be changed because they were not foreseen as part of the overall brief.

The points to bear in mind when briefing are: do you have a specific budget to spend or are you relying on the designer to tell you what your stand will cost; have you given the designer a complete schedule for exhibits, their size, appearance and caption requirements; do you have a corporate style or identification manual and has the designer a copy; do you need office space, storage space for brochures, coats etc.; do you want seating, and for how many; will you 'entertain' on the stand; do you want to sell particular products, the whole range or create a corporate atmosphere within which to sell.

It does not matter whether the information comes from one source in your company or from several. But it will save time if as many facts as possible are assembled at the beginning, without relying on the designer to identify gaps and have them filled by asking questions. It should be made clear from the start to whom the designer is responsible – and that person should have authority to commit the company to money and to policy.

Progress of the work Design work normally passes through four stages, though these may vary, both in length and scope, with particular jobs. They will be adapted to suit the requirements of your commission and explained in detail in the designer's contract letter.

Preliminary design proposals The designer's function is to translate your brief into a solution satisfactory to all concerned. This involves bringing together a number of elements: fitness of the object for its intended purpose; suitability for the manufacturing process; economy of materials used; ease of maintenance; ergonomic and other human aspects; environmental considerations. It is usual for some of these factors to be in conflict with each other and the designer's job is to bring them into balance, ensuring that the end result comes within your budget and is pleasing to the consumer.

This means that even the simplest project calls for detailed consideration of all the factors likely to affect it directly or indirectly. As good design depends on meticulous attention to detail, the first stage of any design commission is usually the longest and most expensive in terms of fees, since it will include all the necessary research in your own organisation, in the designer's office and outside. When the work has been completed the designer will prepare his proposals in visual form for your discussion and appraisal.

In stand design this includes making the best use of the stand's position relative to its immediate neighbours and to the main features of the exhibition hall, including gangways. It will also involve working out how much space you will need on the stand – for the exhibits, for entertaining and sitting, and for storage. Having taken into account all the physical requirements, the designer will also be concerned at this stage with the overall effect, which he is in a unique position to visualise and coordinate.

Development of design proposals Once the preliminary design proposals have been approved, they can be developed as necessary to take account of any agreed amendments, further enquiries or testing, together with the production of models, prototypes, samples, proofs or dummies (according to the type of design). It may well be that this stage is not necessary if the preliminary proposals are acceptable as they stand, although models can be very useful in interpreting plans to clients and in helping to speed up work on site at the exhibition. In addition, photographs of models can be used for advance publicity in the trade press.

Preparation of finished drawings When the proposals have been finally accepted, the designer will prepare all the drawings, specifications, layouts, artwork etc depending on the type of design. He will also obtain estimates and tenders and place contracts on your behalf, particularly for exhibition work, but also if required for printing, packaging and product design. If a model is being used, it is essential to ensure that it is made to the final approved design and that photographs of it are available for your PR department.

Advice on/or supervision of production Your designer will want to ensure that his work is carried through to a high standard in the production stage. This is as much in your interests as his and can be achieved by involving him in an advisory, or preferably supervisory, capacity until the work is completed.

It is particularly important to see that work on site during the build-up period to the exhibition is properly supervised. Ideally, the designer should be available for consultation, but if this is impracticable or too expensive, it is especially important that the plans are clear for the contractor to follow. Adequate supervision and checking of progress on construction may well avoid mistakes when time to put them right is at its shortest. The day before the exhibition opens, you or your designer (or possibly someone in your organisation who is not so familiar with the details of the project) should look objectively at your stand, as though you were a visitor seeing it for the first time. It is surprising how easy it is to overlook the simplest of faults through being too close to the work.

Methods of paying a designer

General Design fees are usually calculated on the basis of the time which the designer estimates that he and/or his staff will need to spend on the work. These can then be expressed in several different ways (some of which are set out below) to suit the particular circumstances of each commission. Alternatively, different methods may be used for the separate stages (e.g. a fixed fee for the first stage and hourly rates for subsequent stages).

Fixed fees The designer quotes a fixed (or lump sum) fee for each stage of the work. To do this he will need to be given a very precise brief. He will also have to make allowances in his quotation for unforeseen problems. On the other hand, you will know from the outset what the total fees will amount to.

Hourly rates Where it is not clear how long a job will take (for instance, when a lot of development work is involved) the designer will quote on the basis of hourly rate fees. You will be charged only for the actual time spent but will not, of course, be able to calculate the total cost of the work at the beginning of the commission. You will however be able to keep a running check on how expenditure is going since the designer will render his account to you at regular (usually monthly) intervals during the progress of the job. Time spent by the designer and his staff will be recorded on time sheets which can be made available.

Fees as percentage of the cost It is usual for fees for interior and exhibition work to be expressed as a percentage of the total cost of the job. The higher the cost budget, the lower the percentage will be and vice versa as design time will not vary much with the quality or size of the stand. The designer will quote the scale to which he works in his contract letter.

Consultancy/retainer agreements and royalties If a client wishes his designer to be available for consultation, usually on a wide range of design problems at policy-making level, he will need to negotiate a fee to cover the amount of time for which he will be expected to be available for meetings, discussions etc. This fee is normally calculated on an annual basis and does not usually cover actual design work. Fees for jobs stemming from an annual consultancy agreement are either negotiated separately as each job arises or may be charged on an hourly rate basis.

Where the client wishes to retain the services of a designer exclusively for himself (normally in a precisely defined area of production) he will need to pay a fee, again usually on an annual basis, to compensate the designer for restricting his activities in this way. The fee may cover advisory services but does not usually include design work as well.

Fees may also be calculated on a royalty basis, related to the expected production run, usually in the consumer goods field. This links the designer's remuneration to the success of the product while reducing the initial cost to the client.

Points to watch

Exhibition stand design Make sure the designer is quite clear about your objectives in participating in the exhibition and knows exactly what products you are trying to sell. His aim will be to draw visitors' attention to the products, not the stand. A brilliant eye-catching stand is desirable but will do its job only if it succeeds in putting across the message about what you are selling. The designer will need to be given the weights and dimensions

of the products, as well as of any furniture or equipment to be used on the stand, since these will be vital components in shaping the overall design.

If you have booked a shell scheme and require only the interior to be designed, there are a number of points which it is equally important to bear in mind: the position of the stand in the hall, whether it is along a wall or is centrally located, and its relationship to the gangways are all vital factors to be taken into account by the designer. He should also be made aware of the Organiser's rules and regulations which may affect the use of special materials in the design and construction of the stand. Fire and safety precautions should be checked to ensure that the stand conforms to them. Once the design has been approved by all concerned (including, if necessary, the Organiser) avoid making any alterations to the designer's specifications since these can prove costly.

Products Some products require an industrial designer, some an engineering designer and some a mix of both. Remember that they were trained in quite different disciplines and so employ their skills appropriately.

Where there is a clear need for an industrial designer together with an engineering designer then discuss the project with them both and ensure that there is a high degree of collaboration from the beginning and that the extent of each work load is clarified, and responsibilities defined.

You may think that your product is so simple or that the function is so important that using an industrial designer is unnecessary. This is rarely true and is a false economy. This history in the UK of companies losing orders to better designed foreign goods is too well known to repeat. Remember that design in respect of a new product or product range is a vital part of your tooling up costs and must be seen in precisely that light. Your slice of the market and the ultimate profits to your company may depend on your understanding of this apparently obvious truth.

So even if the design assistance you require is slight you should still engage a designer to add his talent and not lose the chance to be ahead of your competitors. The stories of the chairman's wife who chooses the boardroom curtains or the exhibition carpet is a joke; the MD who ignores the design of his stand or his product is not a joke.

Graphics You should ensure that the designer is aware of your corporate style and the style that you have established already in printed material; if you wish to break with the style of your current range of literature, you should say so; if you have a preferred typestyle, if the literature is (as it probably will be) categorised by sfb and udc coding and if it fits into a ring or other binding system you must say so.

If you have a restricted budget, let the designer know; he can then work within it. There is no need for escalating costs if the brief is clear. Be clear about the delivery date and place; ask how bulky the order will be, as this will affect transit and storage. Check how much you will dispense on the stand and make sure you do not run out of print during the exhibition. See that you have a supply of give-away leaflets as well as your main brochure – and make sure you give your expensive brochure only to those you know or whose name, function and address you know, The Organiser will give you an idea of the volume of visitors in different categories on different days, so plan your print order and your staffing requirements well in advance.

© 1984 Andry Montgomery Ltd

How to find a designer

The Design Council Designer Selection Service.

There are literally hundreds of freelance designers or group practices operating throughout Britain. Finding the one that best fits your particular needs or circumstances can be a chancy, time-consuming and costly business. The Designer Selection Service can cut through this wasteful process and provide you with a pre-selected short list from our extensive records.

We can help you by matching the special skills and experience of designers on our lists with the requirements of the job to be done. You make the final decision after discussions with the designers whose names and backgrounds we give you.

We recommend individuals or design groups providing services in the following fields:

Product design and development in a wide range of manufacturing industries including industrial design in engineering. Packaging, graphics, corporate identity and all aspects of design in market communications.

Interior design, including exhibition design, display design and industrial model-making.

The Design Council, 28 Haymarket, London sw1y 4su. Tel: 01–839 8000.

RIBA Clients Advisory Service

The normal services of the architect to the construction industry are generally understood but the implications of the architect's design contribution in a wider field are less well-known. Many of the imaginative stands at exhibitions demonstrate the architect's flair for understanding and transmitting the exhibitor's message. That same source is evident in the museums that grace many of our cities and inform their people.

Simple direct terms and 'Plain English' make technical literature far more palatable and understandable to the broad range of people who see it. Many architects create such literature and illustrate it in a way that supports its persuasive character. Nothing is more expensive than technical literature that is ill-understood.

The design of many components and materials with which our best buildings are constructed is also the work of architects, as are also the furniture and fittings which enhance their usage in practical and comfortable fashion. The architect's unique knowledge of the full span of the construction process equips him/her to answer this challenge.

The Clients Advisory Service of the Royal Institute of British Architects gives clients the opportunity to look at the records of architects in their many fields of activities and the service is free. Informed choice is available through this service to all clients whatever their problem by contacting the Clients Advisory Service at 66 Portland Place, London W1N 4AD (Tel: 01–580 5533), or one of the Regional Offices listed in the Yellow Pages.

SIAD Designer's Register

The Designer's Register at The Society of Industrial Artists and Designers provides rapid access to full information on design practices and freelance designers, all of whom are SIAD members. Individual client requirements are carefully matched with the skills, experience and expertise of designers. You may view and compare the work record of designers in complete confidence and with no obligation. Or, if you prefer, or find it inconvenient to come to London, consise information on designers will be mailed to you by return post. You may specify the type of designer, the size of practice and geographic location.

The Register covers all areas of design expertise including: exhibition graphics, product and surface design. SIAD, 12 Carlton House Terrace, London SW1Y 5AH. Tel: 01–930 1911.

Index

Index

Index